OXFORD
AIRFIELDS
IN THE SECOND
WORLD WAR

Robin J. Brooks

COUNTRYSIDE BOOKS

NEWBURY, BERKSHIRE

COUNTRYSIDE BOOKS
3 Catherine Road
Newbury, Berkshire

To view our complete range of books,
please visit us at
www.countrysidebooks.co.uk

ISBN 1 85306 708 3

The cover painting by Colin Doggett shows
a Photographic Reconnaissance Mosquito
pulling away from RAF Benson

Designed by Mon Mohan

Produced through MRM Associates Ltd., Reading
Typeset by Techniset Typesetters, Merseyside
Printed by Woolnough Bookbinding Ltd., Irthlingborough

CONTENTS

INTRODUCTION

Though far from what became known as the 'front line' in the south of the country, the Oxfordshire airfields played a dramatic part during the Second World War in the victory over a ruthless enemy. Oxfordshire's contribution to the war effort mainly lay in the many training airfields that abounded in the county, and the many troops who flew from them during the great assaults upon mainland Europe.

It was for the training of bomber crews and glider pilots that most of the airfields will be remembered. That is not to say that the personnel on the airfields did not see war at first hand. Several of the sites were to receive attacks from the Luftwaffe causing both death and destruction. The repairing of damaged fighter aircraft was also important in the county, an essential task enabling the fighters to return to operations as quickly as possible. Many of the airfields are now just memories but the military still has a presence in the county with Benson, Brize Norton and (for parachute training only) Weston-on-the-Green remaining operational to carry on the great tradition.

It was also a war against the civilian population for the enemy did not distinguish between military targets and civilian towns and villages. Thus the people of Oxfordshire also came to see the horror of war, and they too are remembered here.

I dedicate these pages to all military personnel and civilians who died or were injured in the defence of the country.

Robin J. Brooks

AREA MAP OF OXFORDSHIRE AIRFIELDS

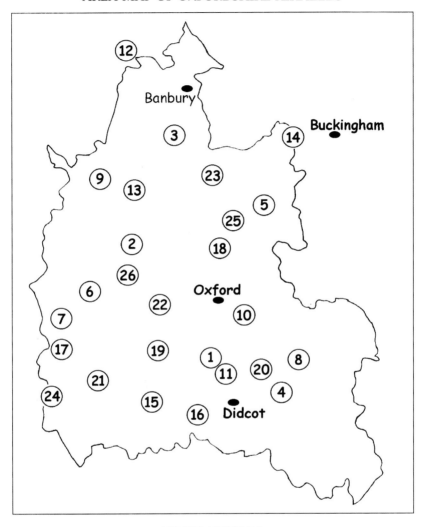

KEY TO AIRFIELDS

1. Abingdon
2. Akeman Street
3. Barford St John
4. Benson
5. Bicester
6. Brize Norton
7. Broadwell

8. Chalgrove
9. Chipping Norton
10. Cowley
11. Culham
12. Edgehill
13. Enstone
14. Finmere

15. Grove
16. Harwell
17. Kelmscot
18. Kidlington
19. Kingston Bagpuize
20. Mount Farm
21. Shellingford

22. Stanton Harcourt
23. Upper Heyford
24. Watchfield
25. Weston-on-the-
    Green
26. Witney

I
SETTING THE
SCENE

The use of aircraft during the First World War altered both the nature of war and public opinion about flight and fliers. Before the start of the first conflict, aircraft were seen to be reserved for those with money and an adventurous spirit. However, by 1918, when it had been appreciated just how deadly a flying machine could be, perceptions had changed. The aeroplane was now seen as a winner of wars, should such a tragedy happen again.

This was of course not thought possible, for when the dreadful consequences of the 1914/18 war were eventually known, it was believed that this was the war to end all wars. There was a drastic cutback in military aircraft production for several years after the Armistice, although the 1920s saw a resurgence of interest in civil flying and aircraft production, so that it became known as the Lightplane era. It was the period of the light aeroplane competitions and rallies, as flying for pleasure became the new popular sport.

Alan Cobham was instrumental in bringing light aviation to the notice of the general public with his countrywide tours. In 1919 his Berkshire Aviation Company came to Abingdon and Oxford to give pleasure flights to all who were interested. During his National Aviation Day display tour in 1932, he visited Banbury on 26th April and Abingdon on 29th April. The 1933 tour saw displays at Witney on 2nd May, Banbury on 9th May and Oxford on 25th May, and both the 1934 and 1935 National Aviation Day tours brought the 'Flying Circus' back to the county.

In hindsight, this resurgence of interest in the excitement and freedom of flight could not come too soon for the future of military

The beginning of aviation in Oxfordshire. Port Meadow in 1918 with No 17 Reserve

Squadron in residence. (Frank R. Cheeseman)

aviation. By October 1924, the slump in the number of squadrons had been reversed. From a total of 25 squadrons in March 1920, the RAF rose in strength to 43 squadrons. Military aircraft production was once again getting started with pioneer companies such as Hawker, Sopwith and Supermarine leading the way. The first non-stop crossing of the Atlantic had been accomplished by Alcock and Brown in a Vickers Vimy modified twin-engined bomber.

Regular air services were getting underway and designs of aircraft were changing. The Schneider Trophy race had become the Blue Riband of all competitive air racing and Britain, after the years in the doldrums, was winning. The 1931 race saw Flt Lt J.N. Borthman complete the course in his Supermarine S6B, a third consecutive British win which meant the trophy was won outright for Britain. It also set new speed records. The design of the S6B was a forerunner to the Supermarine Spitfire, yet at that time, no one expected another aerial conflict to happen. They were indeed very wrong.

The County of Oxfordshire had seen flying when it was in the very early stages. It was Port Meadow, by the Thames, that first attracted the early aviators. One of them, Hubert Latham, a Balliol graduate, landed there on 19th May 1911 in an Antoinette Monoplane after flying from Brooklands. The *Oxford Journal Illustrated* reported the event in glowing terms: 'crowds cheered as the aeroplane glided upwards in a majestic fashion. Higher and higher it went until it was evidently speeding along swiftly for it was soon lost to sight'. Seeing the potential of Port Meadow, the Army soon acquired it for experiments with balloons, airships and fixed wing aircraft. It was used during the First World War as a training area and an airfield. December 1917 saw No 34 Training Squadron arrive and in April 1918 they were joined by No 17 Training Squadron. At the same time, Bicester and Upper Heyford were opened, though with the end of the war they both closed in 1920.

Seven years later thoughts were once again turning to bomber stations in the county and Upper Heyford reopened on 12th October 1927 and Bicester in January 1928. A third bomber airfield, Abingdon, was officially opened on 1st September 1932. In May 1936, No 1 Bomber Group was formed and took control of all three airfields. They were each equipped with the Hawker Hind, a general purpose day bomber developed from the successful Hart. This was an aircraft of the RAFs 'expansion scheme' period during the mid 1930s with a total of 528 being built. It was the last biplane bomber built pending the arrival of the monoplane Fairey Battles and Bristol Blenheims.

Before the big expansion period, this garage was directly in the middle of the then smaller airfield at Benson. (RAF Benson)

By 1936, building of the expansion airfields was at full stretch. Large areas of land had to be levelled and dividing hedges pulled down. Fuel tanks had to be installed, buildings and hangars to be erected. The Air Ministry were only too well aware of public opposition to digging up large areas of land and cutting down trees. In order to appease the objectors, the Works Directorate were instructed to design and build stylish buildings which would blend in with the local surroundings. In the event, most of them were of a similar appearance and had to meet the requirements of the Royal Fine Arts Commission and the Society for the Preservation of Rural England. The airmen's accommodation blocks were usually grouped around the parade ground with the NCOs' and Officers' messes totally separate buildings. In the case of the latter, there was a strong Georgian influence on the design which some of the buildings on the county's operational stations still bear witness to, to this day.

It was Harwell that was to be one of the first of the 1935 'expansion' airfields. It was earmarked as an OTU and served in this role for much of the war. Its squadrons participated in the D-Day landings and in the

11

Arnhem operation, until in 1946, it became part of the then Ministry of Supply carrying out research into the Atomic Bomb. It remains to this day one of the Atomic Energy Research Establishments. Abingdon and Upper Heyford were modernised under the scheme with Brize Norton and Benson being constructed in 1937. Both were used initially in the training role with Brize Norton eventually becoming a major peacetime transport base, whilst Benson will forever be associated with photographic reconnaissance work. Today it is a helicopter base having just received the new Westland Merlin.

Many of the other airfields in the region were given over to flying training. Bicester, from its First World War beginnings, underwent major expansion during the 1930s and accommodated Blenheims during the second conflict. Others used for training were Barford St John, Chipping Norton, Edgehill, Enstone, Finmere, Kelmscot, Kidlington, Kingston Bagpuize, Shellingford, Stanton Harcourt, Watchfield and Weston-on-the-Green. In addition, Barford St John and Edgehill were to see the advent of the jet aircraft at first hand. Some of these airfields acted in the roles of Relief Landing Grounds and Satellites to the larger ones. There was also an American presence in the county with Chalgrove and Mount Farm being given over to American PR operations whilst Grove acted in the troop-carrying and maintenance roles. The Navy was represented by Culham which in 1944 was HMS *Hornbill* and was an aircraft receipt and dispatch unit; there remains some of the best examples of different style hangars in the country, still being used by industry. Likewise, the guard room is in a superb state of preservation and is nostalgia personified.

The remaining units in the county were the Civilian Repair Depots which carried out sterling work on repairing mainly single-engine aircraft such as Hurricanes and Spitfires. These were situated at Cowley, the home of Morris Motors, and Witney. Cowley also played another major role in the war effort with the production of over 3,000 Tiger Moths, many of which are still flying today in civilian hands.

Though far from the main battle area, all of these sites played their part in the final defeat of the enemy during the Second World War. Today just two major military bases remain in the county, Benson and Brize Norton, and in a world of economic indulgence, is their future really assured?

The Building of the Airfields

It was the greatest civil engineering feat undertaken in the United Kingdom since the railways were built a century before. From about 1934, new airfields were being built or old ones were being refurbished and enlarged right up until 1945. It was a complex task carried out by two main military units, the Royal Engineers and the RAF Airfield Construction Service, and by several civilian construction companies.

The dictating body was the Air Ministry Aerodromes Board which was formed within the Air Ministry Works Directorate on 26th May 1934. From this time until the beginning of the war in 1939, the compulsory acquisition of land for airfield building was sometimes hampered by petty procedures incorporated within the Defence Act of 1842, together with the opposition of landowners. In 1939, the Defence Regulations made under the Emergency Powers (Defence) Act, gave the Air Ministry powers of immediate compulsory acquisition of land and buildings thus speeding up the process considerably.

Most of the airfields initially followed a similar pattern with a grass landing area laid to a standard diameter of 1,100 yards. Surrounding this was a circular track with buildings and hangars situated in one area and following the curve of the airfield perimeter. Further expansion was required when the laying of hard runways was done though not all the airfields in Oxfordshire were to have such a facility.

In addition to the refurbished and new airfields that were being constructed during this period, a further class of civilian aerodromes were considered for military use. These were the Automobile Association Landing Grounds.

It was in 1932 that the AA considered extending its courtesy service to the aeroplane as well as the motor car. The *AA Register of Landing Grounds* was first published in October of that year. Usually just a large area of smooth grass owned by a local farmer, the sites were located conveniently close to the large touring hotels. The landowner was paid a small sum to keep the landing ground clear of livestock and to see that the grass was kept short. Petrol could be supplied by a local garage, the proprietor of which was only too pleased to bring it to the landing ground and increase his sales. When the war became imminent, the AA handed all the documentation for the sites to the Air Ministry but few were found to be suitable upon inspection. One

John Laing and Sons were the principal civil engineers in building RAF Benson. (RAF Benson)

14

which was however, was in Oxfordshire at Clifton Hampden. This was requisitioned and became RNAS Culham. The rest of the landing grounds were obstructed with various large items lest an invasion by the enemy gave them access to the sites.

With the expansion scheme came a need for a Lands Officer to advise on the suitability of a site, what extra drainage would be needed and to act as liaison between the military and the landowner. As the work increased so more man-power in this capacity became necessary. Low pay did nothing to encourage the recruitment of such people and consequently, many areas were built upon without being first checked by a Lands Officer. Waterlogging was the main problem with some of the sites. This situation however improved in 1941 when the department came under the auspices of the Treasury and pay was duly increased. In that year, staff numbers rose from 26 to 81.

Many companies were employed on the building of the airfields, among them John Laing, Wimpeys, McAlpines, Taylor Woodrow and Bovis to name but a few, plus the experts on the grass airfields, James Hunter. They employed thousands of civilians on the building pre-war but with the advent of the war, many of the men were conscripted into

One of the measures used to prevent enemy gliders or planes from landing – wires stretched across the road. (SE Newspapers)

15

*A group of airfield construction personnel take a well-earned break during 1938.
(RAF Benson)*

the forces and man-power was to prove a problem. This obviously slowed the airfield building programme which even at this time, was still going on. In 1942, a labour force of 60,000 men were employed on building airfields in the UK alone. The intervention of Ernest Bevin, the Minister of Labour and National Service, decreed that 28,000 men due to be conscripted into the forces were to be deferred to remain in the building industry until October 1942. This gesture, together with a large influx of Irish labourers, once again speeded up the programme.

In March 1941, the RAF Airfield Construction Service was formed, mainly to carry out repair work on airfields that had been bombed. Early in 1943 it was renamed the Airfield Construction Service and was made up of 20 squadrons, two of which were responsible for some of the work in Oxfordshire and are listed below:

16

5008 Airfield Construction – S.W. Midlands. PSP laid in the touch down area at Brize Norton.

5015 Airfield Construction – S. Midlands. Laying PSP runways at Kingston Bagpuize.

In 1942, the construction of new airfields reached a peak of 125 and between 1939 and 1945, 444 new airfields were constructed in the UK. At one period nearly a third of the country's labour force was employed on this work. Repairs to blitzed and damaged private houses was purposely slowed down to allow this huge building programme to accelerate. It remains today, alongside the construction of the Channel Tunnel, Britain's foremost modern civil engineering feat.

Hangars

As far back as the time when the Royal Flying Corps was formed in May 1912, aircraft have used hangars for protection. The early military used a large wooden shed on the permanent stations whilst in the field it was usually a canvas structure. By 1916, the timber-framed Bessonneau was being supplied in large numbers, some of which were still in use in 1939 and indeed survive to this day.

In between the wars it was the Type 'F' Flight Shed that seemed to spring up at many airfields. This was of steel construction with side opening doors and served its purpose until 1924 when it was superseded by the 'A' Type. This was the biggest hangar of the period with a span of 120 feet and a length of 250 feet, opening at both ends. Even this proved too small for the newer, larger aircraft and a new design was submitted and called the 'C' Type hangar. It is this type that can be seen today at many airfields, some of the best examples being at Abingdon, Brize Norton and Benson.

The brickwork incorporated in the hangar was so designed as to fool any enemy as to its true proportions whilst the large windows were intended to absorb an explosion should a bomb come through the roof. With a height of 35 feet, these hangars were built in varying lengths to allow them to accommodate as many or as few aircraft as were required. Though very strong and able to withstand a lot of punishment, they were costly both in quantity of materials needed and

The expansion of Benson begins. The building of the 'C' Type hangars. (RAF Benson)

manpower to erect them. With the opening stages of the war it was felt that speed and simplicity in the erection of hangars had now become essential. The steel firm of Sir William Arrol and Co Ltd came up with the design of the 'J' and 'K' Type hangars, which were able to be built quickly. They were of metal construction with curved roofs of steel plate and many are still to be seen in use today.

There were several more hangars in the alphabet series including the 'D' Type and the 'L' Type. The former came from the Design Branch of the Directorate General of Works whilst the latter was a product of the Tees-side Company. It is however, the Blister hangar that evokes many memories of wartime airfields.

It had been known for some time that it was preferable to disperse aircraft around the airfield perimeter in case of attack, when not undergoing major repairs or maintenance. For their protection and for the convenience of the groundcrews when carrying out minor work, Messrs C. Miskin and Sons produced the Blister hangar. With a prototype being erected at Biggin Hill in Kent in January 1940, three types were offered.

The standard Blister was of a wooden arched rib construction with a span of 45 feet and clad with corrugated iron. The 'Over' Blister was of steel and 65 feet in span whilst the 'Extra Over' Blister was also of steel and 69 feet wide. With a length of 45 feet, they were fitted with canvas curtains at each end but in adverse weather conditions they proved very cold. Consequently, many were either bricked up or steel sheeted at the back end, allowing the poor groundcrews some comfort. Over 3,000 of this type were supplied to the RAF, many of which survive today and are in use for agricultural purposes.

Being an area mainly used for training bomber crews and therefore flying larger aircraft, the Oxfordshire airfields were to have the larger hangars in use. The Ministry of Aircraft Production designs, A1 and B1, were built for bomber aircraft stations and were specialised hangars incorporating work areas along the sides. In addition, many of the airfields were supplied with a design that is still very much in use today. The Air Ministry in collaboration with the Tees-Side Bridge and Engineering Works developed the 'T' Type, this standing for 'transportable'. A sturdy metal construction, the T1 had a span of 95 feet, the T2 of 115 feet and the T3 of 66 feet. 'T' Types can be seen today on many of both the disused and the still operational stations.

No 541 Squadron at dispersal at Benson in 1944. The hangar is an Over Blister type. (RAF Benson)

19

Control Towers

Prior to 1939, the control of aircraft on the ground was sparse and in the air within the airfield circuit, it was nil. Pilots and their aircraft were really only required to book in and out from a building then known as the Watch Office. Even in 1940, it was the Watch Office that controlled the positioning of aircraft on the airfield and their movements. The term Control Tower had not yet arrived. It soon became apparent, however, that with the increasing numbers of aircraft a firmer type of control was needed before accidents began to happen.

The tower began as a single-storey, purpose-built block with a few windows. The Air Ministry were considering, amongst others, a larger building numbered 518/40 which was a two-storey building with access to the roof. However, with the building of airfields continuing during 1941/42, the type 12779/41 became one of the standard towers. This was again a two-storey, brick building with windows allowing the airfield controller a panoramic view of the entire airfield. This tower was redesignated 343/43, a fine example still remaining at Broadwell. Further adaptations of the 12779/41 became 13726/41, which were situated at many training stations such as Chipping Norton.

Many of the Oxfordshire airfields still retain the wartime tower with one fine example in situ at Kingston Bagpuize. It stands as a sentinel to the wartime period.

Domestic and Work Buildings

The expansion period for airfield buildings has left a fine legacy for historians to see. From the guard room when one enters an airfield through to the farthest domestic building, those from that period have stood the test of time. It was the Station Headquarters (SHQ) that basically contained the administration arm of the station. Built to a design labelled 2084/35, the two or three storey building housed the clerical section, pay and accounts and of course, the CO's office. Whilst this was a brick building, being the hub of the airfield, it was heavily sand-bagged during wartime together with having a large proportion of tape across the windows to prevent splinters of glass flying should a bomb drop nearby.

The Operations Room was certified a bomb-proof building which housed the operational nerve centre of the station, command and control of the squadrons and a signal receiving centre. Built of thick reinforced concrete and when shut, sealed from the outside world, the wartime versions served well into peacetime until replaced by more sophisticated buildings.

Technical and accommodation buildings on the other hand, were simple in construction. By the beginning of the war the standard Air Ministry prefabricated hut was the 'B' Type which was given a life span of five years. When, in 1940, timber was at a premium, alternative types were developed. These were constructed of different materials and were given a life expectancy of ten years. The Ministry of Supply Timber Hut, using less timber, was the first followed by the Laing Hut consisting of light timber, plasterboard and felt, and the Maycrete Hut made entirely of concrete. One of the more common huts seen in the First World War was revived and put to very good use, many of them standing today. The Nissen Hut, designed by Colonel P. Nissen, was built in large numbers on most airfields and could be done so in spans of 16, 24 and 30 feet. Other huts in use were the Iris, Romney and the Ministry of Works Orlit.

In addition there were buildings in which were incorporated the various other functions which enabled the station to run smoothly. Station armouries, photography, parachute stores, clothing stores and many others, all were vitally essential. As an indication as to how much value the military placed on station buildings, between 1935 and 1939 the Air Ministry spent £4,500,000 on hutting. A great deal of money for that period.

Camouflage and Decoys

It was in 1935 that the idea and necessity of camouflage was first pointed out to the Air Ministry. It was not however until 1939 that they really began to show any interest. Only when the artist, Norman Wilkinson was appointed an Honorary Air Commodore and told to come up with a camouflage scheme did this vital area of deception begin. It was only just in time for in May 1938, the RAF had just this one officer. By 1942, the department had increased to 330 people.

Camouflage was found to be easier on the grass airfields where it was simple to plant trees and hedges in areas where it would not affect flying. When hard runways and perimeter tracks were built the job became a little more difficult but one solution was to dull the runways and tracks by applying Stadishal Slag Chips. This certainly disguised the concrete but some bomber stations were inadvertently supplied with over-large and sharp chippings which resulted in a lot of tyre damage and generally gave the idea a bad name. Efforts were made to find other materials resulting in experiments with sawdust, wood shavings and even seaweed.

All of these proved unsuccessful for one reason or another but further experiments with tree bark sprayed with an iron salt produced a dark black colour. This was duly tested on the runways at Stanton Harcourt and proved very good, making them invisible from the air. With the first rains however, the mixture turned very slushy, so much so that it proved impossible for aircraft to use the runways. Eventually a wood substance was used to do the job but by 1943, with the war running in the Allies' favour, the urgency to camouflage was not so intense. The operation was to employ 1,000 men, use 22 million gallons of paint, eight million square yards of steel wool and to cost £8,750 per annum. Lucky that earlier thoughts had turned to the ultimate deception, that of Decoy airfields

Though it is not generally known, the British film industry made a significant contribution to the war. An Air Ministry establishment called the British Decoy and Deception Department was created in 1939 under the control of Colonel Sir John Turner. It became known as 'Colonel Turner's Department' and it set up its headquarters at the Sound City Film Studios at Shepperton in Middlesex. It was here they designed and built dummy aircraft, false airfield lighting and buildings, before going out to inspect the planned decoy sites and meet the local farmers and landowners together with the crews picked to man the sites.

It was planned that construction of the sites would be classified by two letters: a 'K' site which had dummy aircraft and buildings for day use, and a 'Q' site with dummy runway lighting to divert night raids. The first sites were ready by January 1940 and such was the faith placed in the idea that by August, 36 'K' and 56 'Q' sites were operational with 406 dummy aircraft in situ. According to the records there were five types of aircraft used on the decoys – Hurricane, Wellington, Battle, Boston and DH Moth. Whilst these were mainly wooden mock-ups, a later idea gave the decoys inflatable aircraft.

The 'Q' sites initially had gooseneck flares laid out at night but this was found to be very time consuming with the amount of effort required to light them every time. These were very soon replaced by Glim electric lights and later by the decoy Drem method of airfield lighting. This was a mock system very similar to the then widely used Drem airfield lighting, named after the Scottish airfield of Drem where the trial experiments were carried out. Like the original, the system consisted of three parts: the runway lighting itself, the approach lighting and the outer circle lighting. Navigational totem pole lights were added to make it even more convincing and if further proof were needed as to the effectiveness of the Drem system, even our own bombers returning from raids sometimes attempted to land at decoy sites.

The other main types of decoy were the 'Starfish' and 'QL' sites. With the enemy bombing moving away from the airfields and onto the towns and cities, they too now came under the decoy plan. The

A dummy Hurricane sits proudly on a decoy airfield in Oxfordshire. (Imperial War Museum - ref. E(MOS)519)

23

'Starfish' sites were an area about one to ten miles away from the main target, deliberately set alight in order to confuse the enemy bombers bombing by night. Known initially as 'Special Fires', some of the larger cities had a ring of decoys protecting them. A similar system was employed on the 'QL' sites but with the addition of lights to help draw the enemy bombers in. Each set of lights was a different colour in order to confuse the enemy into thinking that it could be a large factory or perhaps a railway marshalling yard. In all there were about 400 'Starfish/QL' and 'QL' sites in Britain.

By the end of 1941 only three 'K' sites remained for with the daylight raids becoming less, it was not cost effective to keep personnel on the sites. Lessening night raids also led to a similar run-down on the 'Q' sites and by 1943, most had been closed. The 'Starfish' and 'QL' sites continued until 1944 when at that time, 400 'Starfish', 'Starfish/QL' and 'QL' sites had been operational. The Oxfordshire area came under the control of the British Decoy Area K3 with its headquarters at Mildenhall in Suffolk.

Colonel Turner's Department played a considerable part in confusing the enemy and although the cost ran into millions of pounds, the saving of lives, aircraft, buildings and plant was certainly worth it. All decoy sites were allotted numbers and those in the county are listed below.

No	Airfield	Decoy
38	Upper Heyford	Otmoor
45	Bicester	Grendon Underwood
46	Benson	Pyrton
47	Harwell	Beedon
66	Brize Norton	Chimney
74	Kidlington	Enstone
148	Abingdon	Pyrton
167	Watchfield	Kingston Warren
–	Chalgrove	Golder Manor

This then was the scene in the county as the country rushed to war. Oxfordshire was to play its part fully, and although not directly involved in the opening phase, the Battle of Britain, it was later to take part in the greatest invasion ever. The story of the Oxfordshire airfields' contribution is a large chapter in the country's wartime history.

2
ABINGDON

For nearly 20 years, until the early 1990s, Abingdon was one of the largest maintenance and overhaul facilities in the RAF. With an aviation history lasting over some 60 years, it is sad that economics finally had their say on the fate of this busy Oxfordshire airfield, which played a part in the 1,000 bomber raids of the Second World War and in the Berlin Airlift that followed the end of the conflict.

The original buildings are an aviation archaeologist's dream, some dating from 1930. Typical of that period are the accommodation blocks, with bricks and tiles in a colour appropriate to the area.

Construction began in 1929 with the official opening on 1st September 1932. Though building had begun before the big expansion period of the RAF, Abingdon continued to grow up to and including this period, which is roughly suggested as occurring between 1936 and 1939. One month after completion, No 40 Squadron arrived flying the single-engined Fairey Gordon biplane; this first unit was to remain at the airfield until the outbreak of war in September 1939. They and the station came under the control of the then Central Area in November 1933. One year later No 15 Squadron (later to be designated XV Squadron) reformed at Abingdon with Hawker Harts, the airfield then assuming the status of a bomber base. Within months, 'C' Flight was hived off to form No 98 Squadron who re-equipped with Hawker Hinds, another biplane bomber.

In 1936 began the RAF's expansion period, that was to include work on Abingdon. New buildings appeared and many of the earlier ones were upgraded. Like XV Squadron, No 40 gave up its 'C' Flight in order to reform No 104 Squadron at the base. With all units now flying the Hawker Hind, a developed version of the Hart, the daytime exercises took on a new sense of urgency as the war clouds began to gather over Europe.

Despite these rumblings, the 1936 Empire Air Day was a great

25

success at Abingdon. It gave the RAF the chance to show off its aircraft and tactics should the war ever arrive. Over 2,000 people flocked to the base to see ground demonstrations and flying displays featuring the best of the period's aircraft. Shortly after the Air Day, Nos 98 and 104 Squadrons moved to Hucknall on 21st August 1936, and on 18th January 1937, 'B' Flight of XV Squadron was split off to reform No 52 Squadron, which also moved to Hucknall.

This expansion of squadrons continued as No 62, which had reformed at Abingdon on 3rd May 1937, had as its nucleus 'B' Flight of No 40 Squadron. Crowding at the airfield was relieved as squadrons moved away, but the Avro Tutors of the Cambridge University Air Squadron arrived during July and No 802 Squadron of the Fleet Air Arm brought its Hawker Nimrods and Ospreys into Abingdon in November 1937 before they joined HMS *Glorious*. Yet another flight was born from No 40 Squadron when No 185 was reformed flying mostly Hawker Hinds. The days of the biplane bombers were drawing to a close as the newer monoplane aircraft began coming off the production lines, and it was the Fairey Battle bomber that heralded this era at Abingdon. No XV Squadron received the Battle II during June/July 1938 followed by the similar type for both Nos 40 and 106 Squadrons (the latter Squadron formed from A flight of No 15 Squadron). No 106 together with No 18 Squadron, left for Thornaby during August and September of the same year. Nos XV and 40, however, were to join forces and become a wing of the Advanced Air Striking Force (AASF) which it was hoped would help stem the relentless advance of the German Army through Europe. At the time of the Munich crisis, both units were put on full readiness, but with the return of Prime Minister Chamberlain from his meeting with Hitler, plus the 'little piece of paper' in his hand, the crisis was averted.

More Battles were received during 1938, all the similarly equipped squadrons carrying out intensive training for the onslaught that everyone expected. The last Christmas of peace saw further preparations for war with No 103 Squadron moving over to Benson on 1st April 1939. Despite all the promises, Hitler invaded Poland on 1st September 1939 and once again, Nos XV and 40 Squadrons were put on full readiness. They flew to Betheniville in France the next day as part of the AASF, but would be forced back to England by December 1939 as the enemy pushed ever closer to the Channel coast.

The commencement of war brought many changes to Abingdon. They began with the arrival of the first of the twin-engined medium bombers, the Armstrong Whitworth Whitley, which first entered service with the RAF in March 1937. No 166 Squadron was equipped with them at Leconfield before moving down to Abingdon on 17th September 1939. Converting to the more powerful Mk III in December, a detachment was sent to Jurby on the Isle of Man.

No 166 were joined by the Whitleys of No 97 (Straits Settlements) Squadron at the same time, both units remaining until they disbanded in April 1940 to form No 10 OTU at Abingdon. Operational Training Units trained new crews who had just been awarded their wings, on to multi-engined aircraft to prepare them for flying as a crew in twin and four-engined aircraft, the course normally lasting about 20 weeks. No 10 OTU soon grew to a sizeable unit flying both Whitleys and Ansons. The first operation carried out took place over enemy territory on 21st July 1940 when a 'Nickelling' operation was flown, dropping propaganda leaflets over occupied Europe. Others were to follow with the Mk IIIs being replaced by the later Mk Vs.

With the start of these operations, Abingdon was given a satellite airfield at Stanton Harcourt in September 1940 with 'C' Flight moving across to use it as a night flying base. It was however, the continuation of 'Nickel' operations around this period that gave the crews their first insight into operational flying. It became known as the 'confetti war' for obvious reasons.

With the majority of leaflets having been printed before the war actually started, it is sometimes questioned as to whether Prime Minister Chamberlain, despite his efforts in meeting Hitler, really always knew that war was inevitable. Were the leaflets his way of hoping to stop the conflict by propaganda? One critic of this method of warfare at the time was Air Vice-Marshal Arthur Harris, later the C-in-C of Bomber Command. He felt that the Germans were taking no notice whatsoever of the message the leaflets conveyed, and that they were simply used for toilet paper. The Minister for Air, Sir Kingsley Wood, on the other hand was all for the Nickel drops. Whether or not they did have an impact is still debatable. The 'Nickel' operations provided valuable operational flying experience but they did incur a high cost in aircrew and aircraft losses and No 10 at Abingdon were themselves to lose several good crews.

This period was to remain firmly in the mind of Mrs Joan Sylvester (nee Walmsley), one of a number of Waafs posted to Abingdon.

'Replying to an advert in the *Daily Telegraph*, I was asked to go

ERINNERT IHR EUCH NOCH?

—an POLEN: Es sind nur vier Jahre her—damals marschierten deutsche Divisionen unter dem Schutz der Luftwaffe von Sieg zu Sieg!

—an den FELDZUG IM WESTEN: Hier bildeten STUKAS die Vorhut der siegreich vorrueckenden Panzer-Regimenter!

—an GRIECHENLAND und JUGOSLAWIEN: Das gleiche Bild!

—an KRETA: Entscheidender Einsatz der deutschen Luftwaffe!

DAMALS GEHOERTE DER LUFTRAUM DEUTSCHLAND . . .

In ENGLAND: Unsere Heimatstaedte durch die Luftwaffe «koventrisiert»! Und WIR mussten es mit ansehen . . . Trotzdem wussten wir:
Selbst wenn die Mehrzahl unserer eigenen Flugzeugfabriken pulverisiert wurde—die Vereinigten Staaten werden den Ausfall ersetzen!

SO war es DAMALS . .

An example of the leaflets dropped on 'Nickelling' sorties.

Joan Sylvester pictured in April 1940 when serving as a general duty clerk at Abingdon. (Joan Sylvester)

for an interview at the Air Ministry on 1st April 1940. Two days later I had a letter telling me to report to RAF West Drayton for two weeks training before being posted to RAF Abingdon. It was a month before my 20th birthday. About a dozen of us arrived there, five of us being detailed to report to No 6 Group HQ for duties as General Duty Clerks and the rest being detailed for duties with No 10 OTU.

I remember seeing the Whitleys spread all around the field, some not far from the airmen's married quarters where the Waafs were billeted. They flew out with leaflets on some raids as practise for the real thing. I remember the continuous roar of the engines as they left and when they came back. We were always glad when they returned safely. We also had a few raids on the base one of which resulted in a hit on the Officers' mess, though luckily no one was killed.

There were happier times such as when the Duchess of Gloucester paid us a visit. She was charming to all the Waafs and she actually came into my office, walked past all the men, and stopped at my desk. She asked me what I did and I replied, rather sheepishly, "I am sorry Ma'am, I cannot tell you as it is secret."

A fine body of girls destined for Abingdon in 1940. (Joan Sylvester)

Abingdon 1940 and a visit by the Duchess of Gloucester. (Joan Sylvester)

She smiled sweetly and said, "Quite right." I was certainly relieved. Then there was the visit of the King, for which the cleaning of the camp went on for days. He did an extensive tour of Abingdon which seemed to go on for hours. Looking back, there were certainly happy and sad times for all of us.'

The new year of 1941 saw No 1 Blind Approach Training Flight become established at the base. Using Whitleys and Ansons, the method it used was the forerunner of today's Instrument Landing System, though with basic electronics.

The first enemy aircraft to be seen over Abingdon came on 3rd December 1940, with six bombs dropped. The Luftwaffe returned on Tuesday, 12th March 1941, a day of low cloud but also moderate visibility. There was a little enemy activity during the daylight hours, mainly early morning, but this tended to fizzle out as the day wore on. A major attack, however, materialised once darkness came with Birmingham being the principal target. It was Luftflotte 3 that was responsible, sending 117 crews into battle. Five of these were detailed to attack Midland airfields, and this included Abingdon.

A single He 111 found the airfield during a break in the cloud cover

HM King George VI at one of the Abingdon gun posts in July 1940, and (below) with the CO, Gp Cpt Massey. (Joan Sylvester)

and dropped 16 bombs. The damage was extensive and in addition to destroying a Whitley, the airfield was temporarily put out of action. Some of the bombs had fallen dangerously close to the bomb dump whilst others had severed the gas mains and the main telephone cable. There was, luckily, no loss of life though several personnel were injured. Forty eight hours later, Abingdon was back in action. Not, however, for long as the enemy returned on Thursday 21st March, when aircraft from Luftflotte 3 again found the airfield and dropped 26 bombs. This attack proved even more devastating with seven offices destroyed and the ceilings and walls of a further ten caving in. Yet once again, there was luckily no loss of life.

With the clearance from both raids continuing, 10 OTU got back to business. It now consisted of 48 Whitleys and 18 Ansons. News had also come through that they were to participate in the '1,000 bomber' raids, the brain-child of Arthur Harris who favoured saturation bombing. The final operation order for the first of these large raids was issued on 26th May 1942. It was intended that the operation would be carried out on the night of 27th/28th May or if bad weather

The station intelligence room at Abingdon in 1942. All information supplied by the air crews was processed here. (Joan Sylvester)

33

intervened, on any night up until 31st May/1st June. It was the weather that was to be the deciding factor for Harris knew that he could not send up 1,000 aircraft to fly in cloud.

For a few nights action was impossible but as Saturday, 30th May dawned, Harris walked from his office in the headquarters of Bomber Command at High Wycombe to the underground operations room. The weather over Germany, he was told, was still unfavourable but there was a fifty/fifty chance that the cloud in the Cologne area, the designated target, would be clear by midnight.

'What of the bases?' Harris inquired. 'They on the whole will be clear,' came the answer. If it was no go, it meant postponement for some considerable time. After some deliberation, Harris placed his finger on the chart.

'1,000 plan tonight. Target Cologne.'

At Abingdon and Stanton Harcourt, work had proceeded all day to get the Whitleys ready for the expected operation. With the groundcrews working non-stop to arm and bomb up the aircraft, the aircrews were poring over maps and working out airspeed, wind variation and courses. Then, at 6 pm, came the briefing. As the crews filed into the briefing room, not yet knowing the target, an atmosphere of suspense and expectation pervaded the room. In front of them, the map of Europe was covered in brown paper. With windows shut and armed guards at each door, the Station Commander entered and ripped the brown paper off.

'Gentlemen. The target for tonight is Cologne.'

No 10 OTU were to put up 21 Whitleys manned by the instructional crews and the pupils. For the latter, their only experience of night flying over enemy territory had been the leaflet drops, mainly over the Low Countries. How, it was wondered, would they stand up to the strain and long flying hours of a bombing raid? There was really very little time to think about it as the aircraft, loaded with 500 lb and 30 lb bombs, lined up at Abingdon and Stanton Harcourt to take off and join the main bomber stream.

At the hour of take-off, the entire station staff appeared on the airfield. At two minute intervals the aircraft took to the air. With engines on full power, they slowly faded from view as they struggled to gain height. Nothing further would be heard from them until the drone of engines announced their return.

From 10 pm onwards, squadrons were taking off from 53 bases in England and crossing the coast of France, headed towards Germany.

The sky was black with aircraft as Lancasters, Stirlings, Manchesters, Halifaxes, Hampdens, Wellingtons and Whitleys, carrying their lethal bombloads, flew over occupied countries. In Cologne, people were looking forward to a Saturday night out and a rest on the following day. Little did they know what was about to happen to their lovely city.

The first aircraft were heard approaching sometime after midnight. With the sirens wailing, the city's residents had not taken to their shelters but had come out of their houses to see if it was another false alarm. When they realised it was not, pandemonium broke loose. Leaflets were gently floating down, dropped by the first aircraft. On them in large black print were the words: 'THE OFFENSIVE OF THE RAF IN ITS NEW FORM HAS BEGUN'.

As the first wave arrived over the city and dropped their bombs, those that followed could see many fires burning below. A later combat report gives an indication of just what the attack was like:

'The sky was full of aircraft all heading for Cologne. Wellingtons, Hampdens, Stirlings and Whitleys followed each other to drop their bombs. The twin towers of Cologne Cathedral were clearly visible in the glow of all the fires burning as aircraft circled the flak barrage. So vast was the burning that ordinary fires on the outskirts of the city looked small in comparison. The flames could be seen to be reflecting on the underside of the wings of the aircraft as the entire city burned.'

History records it was a devastating attack, flattening large areas of the city to rubble. Fires were still burning for days after, hindering the job of the reconnaissance aircraft to take photographs of the destruction. As the death and injury toll of civilians reached over 5,000, the total area of complete destruction caused amounted to 2,904,000 square yards. Meanwhile, Bomber Command counted its losses. Out of a total force of 1,046 bombers, 41 were missing. The OTUs however, including No 10, had suffered far less than the front line squadrons, Bomber Command having put up many inexperienced crews who would not normally have been sent against a major target without further training. Of the missing crews, only 17 were from the OTUs.

A message from Winston Churchill to Arthur Harris was circulated to Abingdon and all the other bases involved in the operation:

' I congratulate you and the whole of Bomber Command upon the remarkable feat of organisation which enabled you to despatch over a thousand bombers to the Cologne area in a single night and without confusion to concentrate their action over the target in so short a time as one hour and a half. This proof of the growing power of the British bomber force is also the herald of what Germany will receive, city by city, from now on.'

All 21 Whitleys from Abingdon returned, with just one crashlanding at Manston. Two nights later, No 10 OTU took part in the 1,000 bomber raid on Essen. With 22 Whitleys departing, only one did not return. Though for technical and weather reasons, Bomber Command deemed this attack a failure, a further 1,000 bomber raid on Bremen took place towards the end of June in which, once again, 10 OTU took part. Sadly this time the unit lost three aircraft as once again, Bomber Command deemed the raid a failure.

The 4th August 1942 saw a detachment of the OTU depart to St Eval in Cornwall to commence operational flying. Thirty-three aircraft were detailed to carry out anti-submarine patrols with Whitleys converted to carry depth charges and equipped with ASV radar. They achieved a great deal of success, carrying out 1,862 sea patrols culminating in 16,864 flying hours. Making 55 attacks, they damaged three U-boats and sank U-564.

Back at Abingdon, further bombing raids were carried out on Bremen and Essen, together with Dusseldorf. As 1942 drew to a close, Abingdon personnel reflected on a very busy year. It had brought success for the OTU but also tragedy with the loss of good aircrew and aircraft. Though the tide was slowly turning, 1943 would see a similar pattern being followed.

As the new year dawned, there were several indications that at last the war seemed to be going favourably for the Allies. The 8th Army had begun its offensive in North Africa and by 23rd January 1943 had entered Tripoli. The USAAF made its first attack on Germany when it bombed the docks at Wilhelmshaven, and the remaining German forces at Stalingrad finally capitulated. Disillusioned with the way the war was going, an attempt to assassinate Hitler was made by some of his countrymen. Whilst it failed, it was surely an indication that there was serious discontent within the German military with the way he was directing the war.

All of this, however, had no effect on the day to day operations at

R.A.F. STATIONS
ABINGDON and STANTON HARCOURT

Officer Commanding : Group-Captain C. D. ADAMS, O.B.E.

Christmas Day, 1942

MENU

O

BREAKFAST—08.00 hrs.—09.30 hrs.

Cornflakes	Porridge
	Eggs and Bacon
Rolls	Marmalade
Tea	Coffee

O

DINNER—11.45 hrs. and 13.45 hrs.

Vegetable Soup
Roast Turkey and Stuffing
Roast Pork and Apple Sauce

Roast Potatoes	Boiled Potatoes

Brussel Sprouts
Christmas Pudding and Sweet Sauce

Mince Pies	Biscuits and Cheese

Dessert

Beer	Minerals

O

TEA—16.30 hrs.—17.30 hrs.

Sandwiches

Assorted Cakes	Christmas Cake

Mince Pies

SUPPER BUFFET will be served at the Station Dance
at 20.00 hours.

Dinner menu for Christmas 1942. Considering rationing, the RAF did very well!

Abingdon. By February 1943, No 10 OTU had 55 Whitley Vs, eleven Ansons, three Lysanders and one Defiant on strength. With a fear of overcrowding a distinct possibility, 'A' and 'B' flights were dispersed to Stanton Harcourt leaving 'C', 'D' and 'G' flights at Abingdon. Night training exercises for bomber and defence personnel, codenamed 'Bullseye', were frequently flown together with an increase once again in the 'Nickel' operations. This pattern was to continue throughout 1943 and early 1944.

Though only twin-engined, the Whitley was a sizeable aircraft weighing 21,660 lb when loaded. Sometimes it was to prove difficult to handle when taking off or landing on the grass at Abingdon. After several near mishaps, it was decided to lay two hard runways, the work commencing on 20th March 1944 and ending in October of that year. Whilst this work was in progress, flying was switched to Stanton Harcourt where the normal operation of 'Nickels' continued. No 10 OTU did in fact establish a record in this field of operations when in February 1944, they flew 13 sorties dropping 1,656,144 leaflets.

Despite the hard runways, the unit were to lose their Whitleys in July of that year and convert to the Wellington X. The addition of five Hurricanes to replace the Martinets at the same time once again brought the strength of the OTU up to 50 Wellingtons, five Hurricanes and two Masters. From this time on until the end of the war, they were to continue in the role of aircrew training, finally disbanding on 10th September 1946.

The cessation of the war brought major changes to the base. In October 1946, Transport Command took control of Abingdon, with No 525 Squadron flying Vickers Warwick IIIs. First serving in the transport role in 1943, the aircraft was also used as a VIP transport. Like the Wellington, it was of metal geodetic construction with a fabric covering. A detachment of No 525 was sent to Schwecat directly they arrived at Abingdon, and the squadron disbanded on 1st December 1946 and was renumbered No 238 Squadron. Remaining at Abingdon, it exchanged its Warwicks for Dakotas. Similar types arrived the same month when No 46 (Uganda) Squadron moved in from Manston.

By December 1947 both units had left and were replaced by Nos 51, 59 and 242 (Canadian) Squadrons. All units were flying the Avro York, a large four-engined transport aircraft. Although first designed and flown in 1942, it did not enter service until after the war. With full priority being given to the Lancaster, the production of the York had proceeded very slowly.

Snow clearance at Abingdon. (RAF Abingdon)

A red letter day for Abingdon was 1st December 1947 when long term residents, No 40 Squadron reformed. They too flew Yorks, making Abingdon an all York base. The reason soon became apparent as the Russians blockaded Berlin. It was the aircraft of No 59 Squadron that were the first to leave and arrive at Wunstorf, just outside Berlin on 10th July 1948. They found a city surrounded by 300,000 Soviet troops whilst the Allied garrisons inside the city consisted of barely 2,000 men. The Russians had switched off all power and had cut all land and water access. Two and a half million Berliners faced starvation and death.

The operation to relieve the city began immediately from the surrounding airfields. Three air corridors, 20 miles wide, were introduced and the aircrews were indoctrinated into the strict flying routines, necessary to avoid collisions. Once the airlift began, day after day, night after night, the air was filled with American C-54s, Dakotas, Hastings, Yorks, Sunderlands and many others. It took extraordinary skill to load and fly the supplies, whilst the groundcrews kept the aircraft serviceable, working very long hours in order to do so. It was this dedication that ensured that the Berliners came through their ordeal.

Abingdon squadrons played their part admirably and when the airlift was over, command of the base was transferred from Transport Command to an Army Support role. On their return from Germany, Nos 51 and 59 Squadrons took their Yorks to Bassingbourne leaving No 242 to convert to the Hastings and leave for Lyneham.

Peacetime Abingdon saw a variety of squadrons, aircraft and small units rotate through. The Transport Command Development Unit and the Air Transport Development Unit moved in together with No 1 Parachute Training School. They were followed by No 1 Overseas Ferry Unit flying Valletas, Oxfords and Mosquitos, and in May 1953, Abingdon once again assumed an operational role with the arrival of Nos 24 (Commonwealth) and 47 Squadrons flying Hastings. Heavylift operations were now being carried out with No 53 Squadron replacing No 24 on 1st January 1957.

The previous year had seen No 47 Squadron convert to the Blackburn Beverley, the first squadron to do so. At the time of its

Instruction in landing carried out in one of the Abingdon hangars. (RAF Abingdon)

Abingdon control tower in 2001. A fine example of many post-war towers.

introduction, this was not only the largest aircraft to enter service with the RAF but was also the first British aircraft specifically designed to drop heavy army equipment through rear loading doors. Sadly, only 47 were built for the RAF before production ended in 1958. The Beverley was phased out of service at Abingdon during 1968 but not before a unique flypast of four Beverleys had enthralled the crowds at the 1967 Battle of Britain display.

It was the twin-engined Andover that replaced the Beverley when No 46 (Uganda) Squadron reformed at Abingdon on 1st September 1966. They were followed by No 52 Squadron who, immediately upon reforming, took their Andovers to Seletar. These were the last regular squadrons to use the base for when No 46 left on 9th September 1970 to move to Thorney Island (see *Sussex Airfields in the Second World War*), Abingdon became a major maintenance base. Transferring from 38 Group to the then Support Command on 1st January 1976, the very large and unique 'F' type hangar became the centre for the overhaul of the Anglo-French Jaguar together with the new Hawks and the aging Hunters. The Repair and Salvage Squadron maintained many of the fixed wing aircraft in the UK and overseas and in addition, Abingdon was used by the Chipmunks and Bulldogs of the University of London Air Squadron and No 6 Air Experience Flight.

It was to remain thus until, following cutbacks in defence expenditure, RAF Abingdon was closed in 1992 when much of the maintenance of military aircraft was put out to private tender.

Abingdon today remains as Dalton Barracks with the Army occupying some of the technical, living and married sites and the airfield for storage and exercises, whilst 612 (Volunteer) Gliding School uses the airfield at weekends.

3

BARFORD ST JOHN

There were several airfields in Oxfordshire that during the war, saw the development of new types of engines and aircraft at first hand. One of these was Barford St John.

Work on the concept of the jet engine had begun in the mid 1930s, with the initial test run of the engine taking place on 12th April 1937 by Frank (later Sir Frank) Whittle. In 1939 the Air Ministry issued specification E 28/29 which called for an experimental aircraft to take and test the new jet engine. Glosters took up the challenge and the prototype E 28/29, serialised WH401, was completed in great secrecy and taken to Brockworth airfield for taxiing trials, the first being on 7th April 1941.

George Carter, the chief designer at Glosters, had prepared a detailed study on the possible design of a real jet fighter. In November, the Air Ministry issued specification F 9/40 which was written around George Carter's suggestions. The following year Glosters received an order from the Ministry of Aircraft Production for twelve 'Gloster Whittle Aeroplanes'. These were allocated the serial numbers DG202 to DG213. By 1942, several prototypes had been built and these were test flown at various airfields under strict security. Most of those chosen had to be near the Gloster works, one of them being Morton Valence. Expansion works at this airfield however meant that an alternative airfield had to be used. Barford St John was chosen and DG202 and DG205 were flown to the airfield, to be later joined by DG206. Now named 'Meteor', the aircraft in flying from Newmarket Heath in Suffolk had performed its first cross country flight and thus, had also placed Barford St John firmly in the history books.

Situated south-east of the village of Bloxham, the airfield began its life in 1941 when a large area of grass was designated a Relief Landing Ground to the Airspeed Oxfords of No 15 Service Flying Training School at Kidlington. The SFTS was run on similar lines to the Civil Air Guard training scheme, but was military in all matters and only trained military personnel. With a firm grass surface, the Oxfords would use Barford St John for landing and take-off practice.

With increased usage, it was decided to develop the airfield extensively and the conventional three-runway pattern was built together with several T2 hangars and accommodation. Almost as if German intelligence knew of the expansion plans, the Luftwaffe took advantage of low cloud on 24th August 1941 and dropped six bombs on the east side of the landing area. More of a nuisance than anything, they did little damage and did not interfere at all with the running of the station.

With this expansion, Bomber Command took control from Kidlington on 10th April 1942 and Barford St John became a satellite of Upper Heyford. Eager to use the new facility, several Wellington IIIs of No 16 OTU flew in with the crews making good use of the recently completed buildings.

For five days in March 1943, the sound of the Allison-powered North American Mustang was heard around the local area when Nos 4 and 169 Squadrons brought their aircraft into Barford St John. Part of Army Co-operation Command, the aircraft as a fighter was handicapped at high altitudes by the lack of power emanating from the Allison engine but it performed well in the role of armed tactical reconnaissance. After five days of participating in Exercise 'Spartan', a large scale army/RAF training exercise, No 4 moved to Cranwell and No 169 to Gransden Lodge. The field reverted back to an OTU base, the aircraft of which seemed to fly in all conditions.

Although the airfield was a satellite to Upper Heyford, there were times when it was the busier of the two. For a Waaf in flying control, there was never a dull moment, as Pip Beck recalled in her book *A Waaf in Bomber Command*:

'Next day I heard that I was to go to Barford St John. So were some of the other R/T operators and most of the Met assistants. Not a lot had been happening at Heyford for some weeks but

Barford was busy. I was pleased about the move as smaller stations were usually friendlier and more easy-going. Transport was laid on to take us over, kit, bikes and all which was fortunate as it was a day of heavy showers.

It was 'Salute the Soldier' week at Barford and a dance was laid on in the sergeants' mess the night we arrived. There were certainly a mixture of nationalities at the OTU and I got friendly with an Australian staff pilot named Colin. He was kept very busy with pupils flying both day and night. Noticing that he had the DFC on his tunic, I asked him about it. At first he refused to say anything about it but eventually I got the story.

The target was Hanover, the date 18th October 1943. His aircraft was still over the target, having just dropped its bombs, when it was attacked by a Ju 88 nightfighter which made three attacks. The German pilot was obviously an old hand and concentrated his aim on the mid-upper turret, just about blowing it apart. In this action, the unfortunate gunner was hit in the eye and blinded. The rear gunner's guns had frozen up in the temperature of 50 degrees below and the Canadian gunner had passed out through lack of oxygen; his hydraulics and oxygen supply had been cut off in the first of the nightfighter's attacks.

Colin's aircraft was now virtually defenceless. As the fighter came in again, he threw the Lancaster in violent manoeuvres, finally diving at 400 mph into the darkness. He said that he expected the wings to break off at any moment. In addition, both of the port engines were now out of action having caught fire.

A Ju 88 R-1, but in RAF markings. This aircraft was escorted into Dyce airport in Scotland by Spitfires when its pilot was intentionally intercepted – he wanted no further part in Hitler's war. (E. Brown)

45

Though they were successfully extinguished, they could not be restarted and were now just dead weight. With great difficulty, Colin managed to regain control and with the help of the bomb aimer, continued to fly the aircraft. The next instruction was to throw out everything portable. Guns, bomb canisters, anything that could go had to be jettisoned. This enabled Colin to maintain a height of 6,000 feet but the situation was still very dicey.

Nursing the two good engines, he prayed that they would not sieze up but his determination held and the aircraft successfully made it to Coltishall in Norfolk. The crew held their breath as Colin came in on a wing and a prayer. Using all his strength and skill, the Lancaster touched down gently and rolled to a stop. The crew embraced Colin before they were rushed off to hospital and the entire episode had a happy ending.

Having heard the story, I wondered just who was to know how much guts and glory was represented by a ribbon and a piece of metal.'

New occupants in the form of the Gloster Aircraft Company Ltd had now arrived at the airfield. Afforded the use of part of one of the hangars at Barford St John, the aircraft F9/40, known as the Meteor, led a very cosseted existence. After arriving in May 1943, the conditions had to be perfect in order for the new jet fighter to fly. The first jet aircraft to fly, the Gloster E28/39, was also afforded the use of the facilities at Barford St John. With good weather prevailing, this aircraft managed 23 flights at the base before moving on to Farnborough for further tests and trials.

With both Meteors in situ, a busy test programme began. This had to be slotted in between the training carried out by the 16 OTU Wellingtons. During the lengthy period of development, the manufacture of the Whittle-designed engine was transferred from the Rover Car Company to Rolls-Royce, the jet engine finally emerging as the W.2B/23 Welland which gave 1,700 lb of thrust. This was the power plant that was fitted to aircraft DG205, the fourth prototype, and the one that was finally chosen to power the Meteor Mk 1 when it entered service with the RAF. The trials at Barford St John were conducted in the utmost secrecy with local villagers wondering just what on earth was causing the high pitched howl that was coming from the airfield. When the test flights moved to Morton Valence, the airfield that had been undergoing reconstruction during late 1943, the noise of the

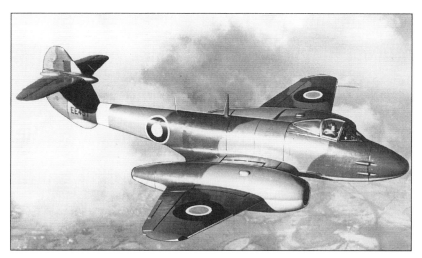

The Gloster Meteor, Britain's first operational jet fighter, was developed at the Oxfordshire airfields. (MAP)

propeller-powered Wellingtons came as a great relief.

Like most of the airfields in the county, Barford St John was also used by many aircraft that were either diverted by weather conditions or were badly shot-up and were unable to make their own base. One such incident happened in late 1943 when 49 B-17 'Flying Fortresses' were diverted to the field due to bad weather at their home base of Podington in Northants. Once landed they were dispersed all around the airfield awaiting their own groundcrews to arrive to check them over before they took to the air again. This of course was marvellous for the permanent personnel at Barford who, in addition to being shown all over the aircraft by the Americans, were also given candies, chewing gum and for the Waafs, nylon stockings. Such luxuries were in short supply for the RAF!

The day after the arrival of the groundcrews, the aircraft were made ready to leave. The aircrews were driven out to their aircraft and soon, one by one, they lined up to take off. Imagine the noise of 49 four-engined aircraft taking off in quick succession. With all the personnel of the station watching, the final one turned and did a last fly-by as a thank you. Life after this episode was certainly going to be a little flat at Barford St John.

On 12th December 1944, flying temporarily ceased for No 16 OTU with the Wellingtons leaving to be replaced by the sound of twin Merlins as the Mosquitos of No 1655 Training Unit moved in. The unit had a combination of the XX, XXV and TIII variants of this famous aircraft. These were mostly built at De Havilland in Canada but in the summer of 1945, they were replaced by the British-built XVI variant. The unit became No 16 OTU on 1st January 1945 and was mainly concerned with training crews for the No 8 Group of Bomber Command. The XVI variant was a development of the Mk IX with a pressurised cabin and was mainly intended for the Mosquito Light Night Striking Force. Some, however, found their way to No 16 OTU.

This type of training continued until March 1946 when the OTU moved to Cottesmore in Rutland. Though by now a sizeable airfield, no further use was made of Barford St John and it was placed into Care and Maintenance shortly after the Mosquitos left. Many of the buildings were gradually taken down and demolished and today the only visible reminder is when you overfly the site and notice the conventional bomber airfield layout. Modern jet fighters, however, owe just a little to the development work that was carried out during the war at Barford St John.

The Mosquito, known as the 'Wooden Wonder'. It served in many roles including photo-reconnaissance. (British Aerospace)

4

BENSON

Situated 13 miles south-east of Oxford, RAF Benson is still operational today. Its extraordinary wartime history is associated with the development of photographic reconnaissance and with the Mosquito aircraft that carried out much of this essential work flying from the airfield.

It really came into existence courtesy of the Automobile Association during 1937 when, in addition to catering for the motorist, they extended their services to the private flyer as well by acquiring large areas of fields and turning them into landing grounds. One site chosen was Wallingford, fairly close to the village of Benson. Wallingford duly opened as an AA Landing Ground but with the coming of war, it became subject to very close scrutiny and inspection by the Air Ministry as to whether or not it could be requisitioned for the military. In the event it was found unacceptable but a nearby site, just outside Benson, was deemed suitable for a major airfield.

Construction began in 1937 during the height of the RAF Expansion Scheme and it took roughly two years for the site to become habitable. Four 'C' type hangars were erected together with domestic and workshop blocks. All of this allowed Nos 103 and 150 Squadrons to fly into Benson from Abingdon and Boscombe Down respectively. Both units flew the Fairey Battle, one of the key types chosen by the Air Ministry as equipment for the rapidly expanding RAF of the 1930s. It was the first of the monoplane bombers and although carrying a bomb load twice that of the biplane Harts and Hinds it superseded, did not come up to expectations. It proved to be under-powered, thus lacking speed and also defensive fire-power.

Arriving on 3rd April 1939, Nos 103 and 150 stayed for five months before moving across the Channel to Challerance in France as part of the Advanced Air Striking Force. The Battle soon proved unsuitable for unescorted bombing operations, as one day in the life of No 150 was to prove when four out of five aircraft were shot down by Bf 109s.

Benson, however, still remained a Battle station when Nos 52 and 63 Squadrons flew in. Included in their equipment were several Avro Ansons, the first twin-engined monoplane bombers to fly from Benson. Forming part of No 1 Pool, the squadrons were joined by aircraft of the King's Flight recently vacated from Hendon.

The Airspeed Envoy, G-AEXX was one of several used by the King's Flight as well as for RAF communications. Shortly after its arrival at Benson however, it was made redundant in favour of a Lockheed Hudson. N7263 had been modified internally and had also been given extra fuel tanks in order to give it further range. Two regular airmen, Sgt H. R. Figg and AC1 L. G. Reed came with the aircraft due to the fact that the Hudson was still armed. It proved not to be the ideal aircraft for the King's Flight and was later exchanged for the De Havilland 95 Flamingo which carried a civilian registration instead of its military one for security purposes.

The arrival of further Battles of No 207 Squadron in April 1940 saw all three Battle squadrons disband and reform as No 12 Operational Training Unit. Armament training was added to the flying training as

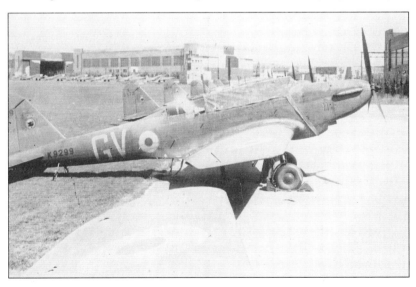

A rare photograph taken in August 1939 of a No 103 Squadron Fairey Battle prior to leaving for France. Note the original control tower. (RAF Benson)

50

Aerial view of Benson around 1940 when it was just a grass airfield. (RAF Benson)

the Battle of Britain was being fought further south. Although far from the main battle area at that time, however, some raiders did make it inland to Benson as the events of 29th June 1940 show. It was a Saturday evening and many personnel on the station were released to enjoy what little recreation they could find. At around 7 pm, the sound of engines were heard in the vicinity of Benson. They rapidly passed but at 11.55 pm, further enemy aircraft were high overhead and dropped 18 high explosive bombs within the area and the outskirts of the airfield. Whilst none landed directly on Benson, several hit the satellite airfield at Mount Farm. This was enough of a warning and the order was given to strengthen the airfield defences.

The heavy losses incurred by the Battles in France meant that there was a rapid turn-over of pilots and gunners leaving the OTU. The 13th August 1940 saw many Polish pilots passing through the training system. The same day there was another attack by the enemy. Around 6.30 pm a lone Ju 88, possibly from the 2nd Gruppe of KG54, dived out of low cloud and dropped four bombs. One high explosive bomb fell on the No 12 shelter which luckily at that time was unoccupied. One Anson was damaged, whilst the remainder of the bombs landed on waste ground. Very little damage was sustained to the base and the

51

training of the Battle crews, now including Czechs as well as Poles, continued uninterrupted.

By this time the Battle squadrons had returned from France and were integrated into No 1 Group of Bomber Command. The Battle's days as a bomber, however, were running out as by July 1940, it had been relegated to a training role.

At Benson, an attempt was made to replace it with a Short Stirling, the first of the large four-engined bombers. With Benson still grass however (a hard runway would not be laid until 1942), the aircraft was found to be too heavy and arrangements were made to bring the Vickers Wellington to the OTU. This too proved heavy and dangerous for night-time flying, but by this time the satellite at Mount Farm had been converted to hard runways. This allowed No 12 OTU to convert to the Wellington and use Mount Farm as its main base leaving just a nucleus for day-flying at Benson.

December 1940 saw the last of the Battles leave, with No 12 OTU converting to Wellingtons, and there was room for the arrival of No 1 Photographic Reconnaissance Unit to fly in from Heston. The activities of this unit were so important to wartime Benson that it is worth looking at its history in some detail.

The winter of 1939/40 had been one of the worst on record. Intense snow showers with freezing conditions brought chaos to all military operations during this opening phase of the war. That is, except to one organisation known as the Aircraft Operating Company and Aero-films. Based in a two-storey building in Wembley, it housed the embryo of a unit that was to become one of the most important in the RAF and one which would help the war effort tremendously. No matter the snow outside, inside it was the work of the eagle-eyed professionals to analyse the many high-altitude photographs taken by an aircraft flown and operated by just one man – Sidney Cotton.

A member of the Air Staff Intelligence named Fred Winterbotham had been a frequent visitor to Germany before the war and, with his position, was able to infiltrate many high places. This enabled him to gather much intelligence material for Britain but with war fast approaching, these opportunities began to dwindle. As a pilot in the RFC during the first conflict, he knew about photographic reconnaissance and had realised the importance of the information good photos could provide. At this point he was introduced to a man by the name of Sidney Cotton.

An Australian by birth, Cotton was already known to the military for his work in designing the Sidcot Suit, worn by the pilots of the Royal Flying Corps. Travelling all over the world photographing sensitive targets, he came into contact with the British Secret Service via Fred Winterbotham. He was approached to see if he would help with a venture to photograph German military targets and after agreeing terms, Cotton said yes. Two Lockheed 12 Electras were made available to him, thereby enabling him to take the most extraordinary pictures.

Soon he had an album full of clarity photographs and on 15th September 1939, Fred Winterbotham told Cotton that Air Vice-Marshal Peck, the Director-General of Operations, would like to meet him to discuss aerial photography. Next morning Cotton presented himself at the Air Ministry and a discussion that would forever change aerial intelligence took place. He was told that two photos were urgently needed of future targets of the RAF. So successful was he in capturing these locations on camera that he convinced Winston Churchill, then at the Admiralty, of the importance of aerial photography.

Given the go-ahead on 22nd September 1939 to work for the military, Cotton formed a unit and was given the rank of Wing Commander (this was in name only as he often flew in civilian clothes). The flight was formed at RAF Heston (see *Thames Valley Airfields in the Second World War*), while the Wembley office, now known as the Photographic Interpretation Unit, was converted to Air Force ways. For security purposes, the entire operation was known as No 2 Camouflage Unit.

Requesting a pair of Spitfires in order to carry out the work, Cotton was at first refused and was given two Bristol Blenheims. These proved totally inadequate and, being Sidney Cotton, he went straight to the C-in-C, Fighter Command, Air Chief Marshal Dowding with the result that two new Spitfires were made available to the flight. With the new aircraft came a change of name to the 'Photographic Development Unit'. It continued the good work through into the new year of 1940 with still further modifications being made to the Spitfires to make them faster. To make interception even more difficult, they were painted in a very pale shade of duck-egg green. Wg Cdr Cotton called it 'Camotint'.

The summer of 1940 was a great time for the unit and photographic intelligence as a whole. It was also a time of change within the PDU as a letter from Sir Arthur Street, the permanent Under-Secretary of State for Air, to Sidney Cotton shows:

'Sir,

I am commanded by the Air Council to inform you that they have recently had under review the question of the future status and organisation of the Photographic Development Unit and that, after careful consideration, they have reached the conclusion that this Unit, which you have done so much to foster, should now be regarded as having passed beyond the stage of experiment and should take its place as part of the ordinary organisation of the Royal Air Force.

It has accordingly been decided that it should be constituted as a unit of the Royal Air Force under the orders of the Commander-in-Chief, Coastal Command, and should be commanded by a regular serving officer. Wing Commander G. W. Tuttle, DFC, has been appointed.

I am told that the Council wish to record how much they are indebted to you for the work you have done and for the great gifts of imagination and inventive thought which you have brought to bear on the development of the technique of photography in the Royal Air Force.'

It was a colossal blow to Cotton although he took heart that his fledgling unit had now become a very important part of the Royal Air Force. Though in no way compensating him fully, the 1941 New Year's Honours List noted that Frederick Sidney Cotton was granted the award of Officer of the Order of the British Empire. The RAF official history recorded that: 'Thanks to the brilliant work of a few individuals, among whom due credit must be given to the adventurous and unorthodox F. S. Cotton, there now existed a means of extensive, efficient and economical air reconnaissance.' He also left a legacy of the same pioneering spirit with which he had so gleefully begun his operations before the war.

The threat of invasion kept the PRU very busy during the long hot summer. By September 1940 the photographs were showing 266 barges at Calais, 220 at Dunkirk, 205 at Le Havre, 230 at Boulogne, 200 at Ostend and 600 at Antwerp. It was obvious that Hitler and his army were ready to strike. In October, for some reason, the photos showed that the number of barges in all the ports had dwindled. As history records, Operation 'Sealion' did not materialise because the Luftwaffe had not cleared the skies of the RAF. The PRU had taken the photos that proved Hitler had changed his mind and cancelled his plans.

Spitfire EN154 of the PRU, Benson 1941. Note the lack of squadron markings. (RAF Benson)

Heston was to receive its first raid in August 1940 but so intense was the devastation from this and several subsequent raids, that it was decided to move the photographic unit to the relative quiet of an airfield in Oxfordshire.

Accordingly, the 'Camotint' Spitfires flew into Benson on 27th December under the command of Wg Cdr Tuttle DFC. To say that the colour of the aircraft amazed the personnel is to put it mildly but with Christmas revelries over, it was back to work with a vengeance.

With the new year came the return of the Luftwaffe, when on the afternoon of 30th January, 19 HE bombs and incendiaries fell inside the airfield boundary but caused little damage. Again on 27th February 1941, an enemy aircraft bombed and strafed Benson, destroying one Wellington in the process. The month also saw several tragedies, the first being on 12th February when an airman was killed when he walked into the revolving propellor of a Wellington at Mount Farm. Training accidents also saw loss of life when Wellington R1285 crashed near Watlington killing two of the crew, and another OTU Wellington crashed near the same site whilst night flying, also killing two of the crew and injuring another.

By March 1941, the number of crews passing through the OTU had fallen dramatically. Bad weather throughout January and February had severely curtailed flying training. On the other hand, No 1 PRU had increased its operations. The Photographic Interpretation Unit had, by early 1941, moved from Wembley to a new home in the Thames Valley. It was a large Tudor mansion called 'Danesfield' and was given the official title of RAF Medmenham. It was to here that the films were rushed from Benson to be developed and scrutinised.

One particular period of intense activity was during March and April 1941 when, in addition to the U-boat problems, the capital ships of the German fleet posed a real threat to Britain. The battle-cruisers *Scharnhorst* and *Gneisenau* and the battleship *Bismark*, became the objects of intense photography from the Benson Spitfires. Because of the distance to be flown to find the ships, detachments of the PRU were sent to St Eval in Cornwall and Wick in Scotland thus allowing the maximum amount of time to photograph the target. Success came on 21st May 1941 when Pilot Officer M. Suckling found the *Bismark* and photographed her in the Atlantic. Landing back at base, the films were

Unidentified PR squadron at Benson with their mascot dog. Note the limited protection given by the Blister hangar. (RAF Benson)

A nice air-to-air photograph of a Spitfire of the PR Unit at Benson. When the unit was broken up into squadrons, the aircraft flew without identity numbers, unlike LY shown here. (RAF Benson)

rushed to be developed with the result that a chase by the Royal Navy for six hours ended with the *Bismark* being sunk. Suckling was recognised as a hero but sadly was lost two months later when he failed to return from a sortie, the first pilot of the PRU to die in action.

As the pace of photographic reconnaissance increased, the number of sorties in April totalled 55. May and the better weather proved even better with a total of 79. Up until this time the reconnaissance Spitfires had only been able to take vertical photos. Now it was felt that low altitude oblique close-ups of targets would help identify targets and so a further version of the Spitfire was developed, the PR1E. This aircraft, of which only one was produced, had a single F.24 camera under each wing housed in a bulging mounting. The first sortie with the new cameras was flown by the CO, Wg Cdr Tuttle, but cloud cover forced him to return without taking the photos.

The next sortie was flown by F/O Alastair Taylor who found the cloud base over his target, the French coast near Boulogne, down to 700 feet. Coming below the cloud cover, he switched on the starboard camera and photographed the harbour at 300 feet. Turning, he repeated the process with the port camera and heading for the English coast, landed back at Benson. When the films were developed at Medmenham, they showed astonishing clarity from different angles, something that could not have been achieved with just the vertical cameras.

The complement of Spitfires in the PRU around this time stood at eight type Bs, three type Cs, two type Ds, one type E and several type Gs. The Gs had lost the familiar 'Camotint' colour and were now painted in a very pale shade of pink. Several Glenn Martin Marylands had arrived at Benson during June to be fitted with cameras. They were intended for Malta where a very able officer named Adrian Warburton was shortly to make a name for himself in the history of photo-reconnaissance flights.

Meanwhile No 12 OTU, still at Mount Farm and Benson, in addition to training crews were now employed on Operation 'Nickel', the dropping of propaganda leaflets over enemy territory. The first 'Nickelling' sorties had been carried out by Bomber Command directly after the declaration of war. Although freely distributed to the enemy, the leaflets were regarded as highly secret when it came to transferring them from the stores to the OTUs. When the bundles were opened, they were loosely fed into the flare chute so that once released, they would separate in the slipstream and be widely scattered. The leaflets would attempt to point out to the enemy the stupidity of their actions as well as containing propaganda material.

This method of warfare did have its effect as a notice to the German people early in 1941 implied. The notice came from Heinrich Himmler:

'Leaflets or other publications dropped by the enemy, as well as other publications of all kinds directed against the State, distributed to disquieten the population or to affect its wartime morale, must immediately be surrendered to the nearest police station. Everyone coming into possession of such a publication is in duty bound to surrender it. Anyone acting contrary to this decree will be sentenced to prison under Section 92B of the Reich Penal Code'.

For most of the aircrews at No 12 OTU, leaflet dropping at night was their first experience of flying under operational conditions. With a crew usually staying together throughout their tour, they came to

Benson station crest. (RAF Benson)

depend on each other as in no other theatre of war. The Wellington, whilst it was a tough and durable aircraft, was also very cold with the only heating coming from water. When the aircraft reached a height of about 8,000 feet, the cold became intense and the only warmth came from one's own body and thick clothing. Then there were the enemy guns and flak to contend with. Earlier on, it had been seen that small numbers of bombers flying in daylight without escorts were easily shot down by the enemy. Thus, most 'Nickelling' operations carried out by 12 OTU and many others were at night.

It was time for several changes at Benson. No 12 OTU, the long term residents at Mount Farm and Benson, moved to Chipping Warden in Northamptonshire on 10th July 1941, leaving the airfield to the PRU. Three days later the first De Havilland Mosquito arrived at Benson.

To many, the De Havilland Mosquito was the most successful aircraft of World War Two. It ranked with the Spitfire and the Lancaster among the most outstanding aircraft ever. Its versatility was unbeaten for it performed in the roles of fighter, bomber and reconnaissance. It was the fastest aircraft in the RAF from September 1941 until early in 1944 and in the bomber role was the fastest bomber until the advent of the English Electric Canberra, the first jet-powered bomber. Little wonder then that it obtained the title of the 'most magical aircraft'.

Regarding the PR version, the last of the three prototypes to fly, W4051, was the first Mosquito to arrive. Making its first flight on 10th June 1941, it now arrived to take up its duties with No 1 PRU. Coded LY-U, it was flown in by Geoffrey De Havilland and landed amidst cheers and clapping for this was the aircraft the PRU had been waiting for. The first sorties were, however, carried out from Wick in Scotland and not Benson.

No 3 PRU which had been stationed at Oakington, now flew in to Benson to join No 1. They brought with them five Spitfires and a Blenheim IV to strengthen the unit as the airfield once again was enveloped within Coastal Command.

The RAF Film Production Unit was formed at Pinewood Studios for the purpose of recording all aspects of operations carried out by the RAF. Previous film had been taken by a civilian concern acting under the auspices of the Ministry of Information, but it was now felt that a military unit would do the job better with the military mind in charge. This became a lodger unit at Benson on 20th September 1941 when a single aircraft, a Bristol Beaufort, was delivered. Further requests for more Beauforts fell upon deaf ears though the unit later did acquire a Hudson and several Ansons.

The first sortie with Mosquitos took place on 17th September when Squadron Leader R. F. Clerke photographed Bordeaux, La Pallice and Brest. Regarding the latter, throughout the autumn and winter of 1941, over 700 photographic sorties were flown over the harbour. The photos showed both German battle-cruisers *Scharnhorst* and *Gneisenau* and the *Prinz Eugen* still in harbour but cosseted by a flotilla of destroyers, torpedo boats and many other protective craft. A new squadron, No 140, had reformed at Benson on 17th September and they too were employed in keeping watch on Brest. Their Spitfires added much to the collection of photos but neither they nor No 1 PRU could ever have foreseen what was about to unfold.

It was known at this time that the German ships could not stay in Brest indefinitely for they were needed by the German navy in the Atlantic to begin their plundering of Allied ships. There were two routes they could take. One was up and around the top of Scotland and the other was through the English Channel. The Admiralty were well aware that the enemy needed his ships to leave Brest at the earliest possible time. What they did not think he would do was to sail close to the shoreline under the nose of the British forces.

Over the Christmas period and into the new year, the watch continued. Then on Sunday, 8th February 1942, two pilots from St Eval took photos of Brest showing that the 'ready to sail' preparations were well advanced. Coastal Command sent an urgent signal to all groups as well as the other RAF commands. Something was about to break. The following day thick cloud obscured the area and no photography was possible. On Wednesday, 11th February, two Benson Spitfires took photos showing the ships were still there. This was the last sortie of the day but before midnight, the fleet had moved out of Brest and were under way. Not to Scotland but into the English Channel. By the morning of the 12th, the ships were steaming through the Dover Straits.

It was a shock to the whole country as well as to the various military departments. A series of mishaps had prevented the British from realising what was happening until the *Scharnhorst*, *Gneisenau* and *Prinz Eugen* were safely through. *Scharnhorst* did in fact strike a mine in the open sea, but this did nothing to suppress the anger and the humiliation that a German fleet could sail along the English coastline

Pilots and aircraft of an unidentified PR squadron at Benson, circa 1942. (RAF Benson)

and not be detected. The repercussions of such an action continued to rumble for many years after.

On 15th May 1942, Flt Lt D. W. Steventon was airborne in his Spitfire high above the Baltic. Flying over the island of Usedom, he noticed an airfield at the northern tip of the island with a lot of new development close by. Thinking it to be of interest, he switched on his cameras and flew over and alongside the target. Upon landing back at Benson, the films were rushed to Medmenham for processing. One of the Waafs on duty that night was Constance Babington-Smith. Comparing on the map exactly where the photos had been taken, she noticed a town by the name of Peenemunde. She had also noticed some new and strange circular embankments but was not specifically looking for anything sinister. The photos were duly filed and placed upon a shelf in the library and forgotten for the next seven months. They were, however, to prove crucial at a later phase of the war.

In Germany, work was progressing on a far more sinister type of warfare indeed with the development of rockets. At Peenemunde, the photos of which were still on the shelf at Medmenham, Wernher von Braun and a host of technicians were about to launch their first A4 rocket. Later to be known as the V-2, the tests were proving very successful as were the test firings of a flying bomb, later to be known as the V-1. At this moment in time however, the secret remained with the enemy.

The King's Flight now prepared to leave Benson to become absorbed into No 161 Squadron based at Newmarket. With very little use of the Flamingo, it was returned to No 24 Squadron. The disbandment of the unit was on the strict orders of the King himself and it was to be another four years before it was to reform, once again at Benson.

Benson's aircraft were by now roaming far and long. In May 1942, No 140 Squadron moved into Mount Farm leaving a detachment at Benson and St. Eval. They had recently converted to the Spitfire IV from the Mark II and had found with additional fuelling totalling 133 gallons, it had an increased range with a top speed of 372 mph compared to 357 mph on the Mark II and a ceiling of 39,600 feet compared with 37,200 feet.

The long awaited building of a concrete runway took place at Benson at the end of May 1942. Though promised early in the war, fighter command bases had taken priority and it was the arrival of the heavier Mosquitos that had really forced the issue. Now the airfield would be able to accommodate any aircraft of the period.

INSTRUCTIONS

(1) Learn by heart the Russian phrase "Ya Anglichánhin" (means "I am English" and is pronounced as spelt).

(2) Carry this folder and contents in left breast pocket.

(3) If you have time before contact with Russian troops, take out the folder and attach it (flag side outwards) to front of pocket.

(4) When spotted by Russian troops put up your hands holding the flag in one of them and call out the phrase " Ya Anglichánhin. "

(5) If you are spotted before taking action as at para 3 do NOT attempt to extract folder or flag. Put up your hands and call out phrase "Ya Anglichánhin". The folder will be found when you are searched.

(6) You must understand that these recognition aids CANNOT be accepted by Soviet troops as proof of bona fides as they may be copied by the enemy. They should however protect you until you are cross questioned by competent officers.

Я англичанин

" Ya Anglichánhin " (Pronounced as spelt)

Пожалуйста сообщите сведения обо мне в Британскую Военную Миссию в Москве

Please communicate my particulars to British Military Mission Moscow.

Reverse side of a transparent silk flag known as a 'Blood Chit' and given to all PRU pilots in case of being shot down or landing in Russian territory. (Flt Lt J. Robson)

Around this time it was decided by the Air Ministry that all PR flights would be upgraded to squadron status. This became official on 18th October 1942 when the Mosquitos of H and L flights became No 540 Squadron and the 14 Spitfire IVs of B and F flights became No 541 Squadron. A further 19 Spitfires of A and E flights became No 542 Squadron whilst 15 others were redesignated No 543 Squadron. Finally, No 544 Squadron was left with a collection of Ansons, Spitfires, Marylands and Wellingtons.

Benson was now a very busy station and in turn, the amount of photos being taken turned Medmenham into a very busy interpretation unit. Much of this work was carried out by Waafs, among whom were Sarah Oliver, daughter of Winston Churchill, Ann McKnight-Kauffer, Eve Holiday and Constance Babington-Smith. The plans for the North African landings brought another hectic time for both establishments when photographic intelligence was called upon to provide a mass of material for forward planning and briefing. All of this meant that Benson was sending many aircraft on detachments, both here and overseas.

*Pilots and groundcrew of No 544 Squadron ahead of one of the PR Mosquitos.
(RAF Benson)*

The night of 16th/17th May was given over to No 617 Squadron –
the Dambusters – from Scampton in Lincolnshire who successfully
breached the Mohne and Sorpe dams. Well documented in many other
books, not so well known is the fact that early the next morning, F/O F.
G. Fray of 542 Squadron left Benson in Spitfire IV EN343, to
photograph the damage. The result was spectacular, with large areas
of the Ruhr Valley flooded. During the next two days, further PR flights
left Benson to cover the extensive flooding.

It was back in December 1942 that reports had begun filtering
through to London of 'secret weapon trials' in the Baltic. Whilst
something was known of the weapons, without photographic evidence
much of this had merely been filed for future reference. Further sorties
over Peenemunde, however, had produced the same alarming photos
showing a lot of activity. One particular operation took place on 23rd
June 1943 when Flt Sgt E. P. Peek had flown his Mosquito high over the
area and in the bright sun had obtained photographs of the utmost
clarity.

These photographs combined with the previous ones were presented
to the Chiefs of Staff who suddenly began to take an interest in what

Immediately after the dams raid in 1943, the PR squadron at Benson were over the target taking the first pictures. This is the breached Mohne Dam. (Public Record Office)

was happening at Peenemunde. Mr Duncan Sandys, then Joint Parliamentary Secretary to the Ministry of Supply, was appointed as senior investigator and with this, the search for secret weapons began in earnest. Aircraft from Benson were constantly over the area throughout June and July, with the interpreters at Medmenham working all hours to see just what was happening. For Constance Babington-Smith, the long hours brought rewards for on 23rd June, after being briefed to look for 'anything queer', she found four little

A pilot and navigator discuss a sortie beside a No 544 Squadron PR Mosquito.
(RAF Benson)

tailless aeroplanes taking to the air. She had found the Messerschmitt 163, a liquid-fuel rocket fighter. This was enough to convince Duncan Sandys that Peenemunde should become the target of our bombers.

The operation of detecting the secret weapons was given the code-name 'Bodyline' and by the autumn of 1943, the building of ski ramps in the Pas-de-Calais had been photographed by aircraft from Benson. These were the launch sites for the V-1 or 'revenge weapon' as Hitler had named it. Further photos showed small black objects at the bottom of the ramps and by November it had been established just what they were. The threat of a cross-Channel flying bomb had become fact.

All the sites immediately came under attack from Bomber Command and the United States Eighth Air Force and were code-named 'Crossbow'. Whilst all these deliberations about secret weapons were taking place, October 1943 saw No 543 Squadron disband at Benson for the duration of the war. Before they did so, B flight formed the nucleus of No 309 Ferry Training and Aircraft Despatch Unit which was to train pilots for ferrying PR Spitfires overseas.

Christmas 1943 and into the new year of 1944 saw the PR work continuing with the remaining squadrons. The talk now was of an invasion of Europe and daily sorties were photographing the coast of Northern France. Nos 540 and 544 Squadrons had by early 1944 received the first pressurized high-altitude Mosquito XVI. This was the ultimate Mosquito for PR work, the total production figure reaching 432. Not to be outdone, the Spitfire squadrons at Benson received the Griffon-engined PR Mk XIX Spitfires. Later versions of this mark also had pressurized cockpits giving it a ceiling of 43,000 feet with a range of 1,550 miles.

The period prior to D-Day was hectic for the Benson squadrons. In order to give the Allied troops the best possible chance of securing a foothold in Europe, photographs of enemy positions were necessary. At the same time the sorties connected with 'Crossbow' continued and by the beginning of June, 68 sites and ski ramps had been identified, all of them pointing towards England. Intense activity around these sites could be seen and it was decided to issue a new code-name for an imminent attack. It was called 'Diver' and was none too soon for in the early hours of 13th June 1944, the first V-1 came down at Swanscombe in Kent. Operation 'Diver' had begun and four of them were to come down in Oxfordshire, beginning with two on 21st June 1944.

The PR operations room, Benson. (RAF Benson)

A Mosquito of No 540 Squadron pictured at Benson in 1944. (Imperial War Museum – ref. P019016)

D-Day took place on 6th June and a few weeks before, Benson had become the home of a joint committee to co-ordinate all the PR activities, both British and American. The squadrons resident at the airfield were now part of a newly formed British Photographic Reconnaissance Group under the command of Air Commodore John Boothman, winner of the 1931 Schneider Trophy race. It was still however business as usual when in the afternoon of 25th July 1944, Flt Lt A. E. Wall and his navigator, F/O A. S. Lobban, took off from Benson in a Mosquito to photograph targets near Stuttgart. After several hours, they had not returned and everyone back at base feared the worst. It was a time for jubilation when a signal was received saying that they had landed in Italy and were safe.

With the Allied landings a success, plans were in hand to hopefully end the war sometime during 1944, with an operation code-named 'Market Garden' fully backed by Field Marshal Sir Bernard Montgomery. It was a bold and imaginative plan but rather impractical due to the fact that troops would have to advance through the flat fields of Holland which were still festooned with enemy troops. In addition, if the plan was to work at all, the bridges across the Rhine would have to be seized by paratroops. It fell to No 541 Squadron to fly with a fighter

*Flt Lt Robson pictured with his Spitfire XI of No 541 Squadron, Benson 1944.
(Flt Lt J. Robson)*

RAF Benson operations room at the end of the war. (RAF Benson)

sweep over the area and take photos of the landing zone. When they were processed at Medmenham, they clearly showed two SS Panzer divisions in the process of rearming directly in the dropping zone.

Despite this clear evidence, the operation went ahead and turned out to be a disaster with terrible consequences. Of nearly 10,000 British paratroopers dropped, 1,130 were killed, 6,500 were captured and just 2,163 were rescued. Why did this happen when aircraft from Benson had taken clear and concise photos showing German troops in the area? It has been said by historians of Arnhem that a decision had been taken by a higher authority that this was Montgomery's plan and that it should be allowed to go ahead whatever the circumstances. When the number of deaths, prisoners and casualties became known at Benson, many wondered just what use the risking of their lives to get the photographs was if they were not to be acted upon. Like the Channel Dash and the Dieppe operation, the arguments regarding the decision to go ahead with 'Market Garden' continue to this day.

Thus, the war was not to end in 1944 as predicted by Montgomery, but was to rage for another six months. Over that period, the PR flights

71

from Benson continued and No 541 Squadron were to be in the thick of it, as Flight Lieutenant J. Robson recalled:

'541 certainly had a mix of nationalities. There were Belgians, South Africans, New Zealanders, Australian, Canadian, Irish, Scots and even a yankee Colonial. We all preferred the Spitfire XI, it cruised at 360 knots and had, with drop tanks, some 5+ hours endurance. The XIX mark was faster but it used to eat fuel and it was a little heavier on the controls.

We were now coming into contact with the Luftwaffe jet aircraft quite often and one of the first pilots to encounter one was an Irishman, Johnny Darling. He was over Munich at about 22,000 feet when he saw a Me 163 take off from the ground leaving a big rocket exhaust trail and coming up vertically. After about 50 seconds it was above him coming in, in a shallow dive. Johnny cut his throttle and dived vertically down to 19,000 feet and the Me 163 pulled away, circled and made another shallow dive. This time

Flt Lt Robson and Flt Lt Adams with a Spitfire of No 541 Squadron at Benson. Flt Lt Adams was killed in 1945 when his aircraft hit the ground near East Grinstead, Sussex. (Flt Lt J. Robson)

The post-war Ferry Squadron at Benson at an annual inspection. Aircraft from left to right are the Meteor, Anson and Valetta. (RAF Benson)

Johnny thought, 'I'll lose you', so another vertical dive to about 5,000 feet and he lost him. Others were not so lucky and fell foul to this very potent new jet fighter.'

Even after Victory in May 1945, photographic sorties were flown daily to assess the damage done to Europe so that reconstruction could begin as quickly as possible. No 542 Squadron disbanded on 27th August 1945 followed by No 544 on 13th October. Nos 540 and 541 were to survive for just under a year until they too disbanded on 30th September 1946. From the remnants came No 58 Squadron equipped with the long range Mosquito PR 34s and two marks of Avro Anson. A past squadron formed at Benson on 1st November 1947 when No 540 reformed from the Mosquito element of No 58 Squadron.

In peacetime, the base continued its PR duties. It heralded in the jet age when English Electric Canberra PR4s equipped 540 Squadron and No 541 received Meteor PR4s before leaving for Germany. By March

A post-war (1949) photograph of an open day at Benson. Aircraft seen are the Tiger

Moth, Spitfire, Proctor and Vampire. (RAF Benson)

The PR Spitfire gate guardian is placed in position. (RAF Benson)

1953, transfer to RAF Transport Command had brought No 30 Squadron operating Vickers Valettas, joined later by Nos 147 and 167 (Gold Coast), both of which formed the Ferry Squadron in 1953. For a brief period in the mid 1950s, Benson hosted the Supermarine Attackers and Hawker Sea Hawks of Nos 1832 and 1836 Squadrons of the Royal Naval Volunteer Reserve.

At this time the airfield received the then new work-horse of Transport Command, the Whitworth Gloster Argosy. The first aircraft reached the OCU at Benson in November 1961, followed by the forming of No 114 Squadron in February 1962. Further squadrons used the base flying the Argosy, among them Nos 105, 267 and 215, before Benson's troop carrying and freight role ended in 1971.

At the cessation of hostilities, the King's Flight had reformed, becoming the Queen's Flight on the death of the Monarch. It later moved to Northolt where it remains today as No 32 The (Royal) Squadron.

Benson has survived the drastic military cuts brought in under 'Options for Change' and is at this time fully operational with No 33 Squadron flying the Puma HC1 helicopter and the Oxford University Air Squadron flying the new Grob 115E Tutor. No 606 (Chiltern) Squadron of the Royal Auxiliary Air Force provides part-time back-up to the regular service and air experience flights for Air Cadets are provided by No 6 Air Experience Flight also flying the Grob Tutor. Just recently established at Benson is the £100 million Medium Support Helicopter Aircrew Training Facility for training many of today's pilots. A new chapter opened in Benson's history on 7th March 2001 when the first four Merlin helicopters arrived to serve with No 28 Squadron. Part of the new Joint Helicopter Command, the aircraft offers a new capability in rapid deployment operations.

Thus Benson's continuance as a major military base is assured, but it will always be recognised and remembered as the home of Photographic Reconnaissance during the Second World War.

5
BICESTER

It was on 25th June 1936 that the prototype of a new twin-engined monoplane bomber/fighter first took to the air. It was a military development of the Type 142 (K7557) that was known as 'Britain First' and which was presented to the nation by Lord Rothermere. One of the new monoplanes ordered under the expansion scheme, it was a great step forward from the biplane bombers and fighters such as the 180 mph Hawker Hind. Designed to Military Specification B.28/35, the Air Ministry ordered the aircraft directly from the drawing board with the first contract for 150 being placed in August 1935.

Known as the Bristol Blenheim, a total of 1,552 Mk Is were produced. Not all came from the Bristol works for the manufacture of this new aircraft was sub-contracted to various companies such as Rootes, the car people, and also the Avro Aircraft Company. It served in many squadrons throughout the war and at many military bases. One of the latter was Bicester, which began a long association with the type in 1939.

The airfield however had already seen service in the first conflict, when it came into use in 1917. No 118 Squadron arrived from Netheravon on 7th August 1918 to disband one month later. Replaced by No 2 Squadron for a short period, the Bristol fighters of No 5 Squadron returned from France to Bicester, this unit also disbanding on 20th January 1920. Two months later, with the rapid rundown of the military following the armistice, Bicester was declared surplus to requirements and closed.

The resurrection began in 1925. Two hangars were constructed, one on the south-west side and the other on the south-east. A special feature, so far as Oxfordshire airfields was concerned, was the building of a railway track which was laid around the perimeter of the airfield finally ending up at the main stores. Additional buildings included an airmen's mess, barrack blocks and technical buildings.

With building complete, the Hawker Horsleys of No 100 Squadron flew in from Spitalgate on 10th January 1928. An early biplane bomber, its main claim to fame was that in May 1927, Flt Lt C. R. Carr and Flt Lt C. E. M. Gillman attempted to fly a Horsley from Cranwell to India. They were forced down in the Persian Gulf after flying 3,420 miles in 34 hours, an unofficial long-distance record. By the then standards already obsolete as an effective bomber, No 100 Squadron took them to Donibristle in November 1930 and exchanged them for the equally obsolescent Vickers Vildebeeste.

As they left, so No 33 Squadron flew their Hawker Harts in to Bicester from Eastchurch in Kent. One of the most adaptable biplanes to ever serve in the RAF, 33 Squadron had been the first to get the Hart whilst at Eastchurch. They worked the type up to a very good standard of flying and at the RAF Hendon Air Display of 1933, a wing drill by three squadrons, including No 33, thrilled the crowds with their precise manoeuvres. From the beginning, the importance to the service of the Hendon Air Displays was recognised. It was realised that this was the RAF's public showpiece and that it must display a blend of showmanship, colour and professionalism. No 33 remained at Bicester for four years before moving to another Oxfordshire airfield, Upper Heyford.

One of the more interesting squadrons at this period was No 101. They arrived on 1st December 1934 and were equipped with the Boulton and Paul Sidestrand. This aircraft dated from 1926 and was a descendant of the Bourges and Bugle twin-engine bombers. For a large bomber it was hugely successful in that it could be looped, spun and rolled easily despite its rather ugly and ungainly appearance. The total production for this aircraft was only 18 with the last being delivered in 1933. The entire RAF allocation went to No 101 Squadron who flew them at Bicester for six months. They then said goodbye to the Sidestrand and converted to the Overstrand. Similar to its predecessor, it had the advantage of more powerful engines in the shape of the Pegasus which gave it increased power and a larger bomb load. Both the Sidestrand and the Overstrand were somewhat grotesque to look at but did make three appearances at the Hendon RAF displays in 1935, 1936 and 1937, always in the capable hands of No 101 Squadron.

On 25th November 1935, 'C' Flight of No 101 became the nucleus of a new squadron, No 48. They quickly moved to Manston whilst

Bicester joined the Western Area and No 3 Group in April 1936. Transfer to No 1 Group on 17th August 1936 indicated that the signs of a war fast approaching were becoming more evident. Further expansion came once again when No 101 Squadron gave up its 'B' Flight to form No 144 Squadron on 11th January 1937. They took over some of the Overstrands but quickly converted to the Avro Anson, taking them to Hemswell on 9th February 1937.

During the prolonged stay of No 101 Squadron at Bicester, the expansion scheme for airfields got underway. Two large 'C' Type hangars were constructed together with further accommodation blocks, married quarters and a pseudo-Georgian Officers' mess. It was obvious that with the deteriorating situation in Europe, the airfield was getting ready for its war. So too were No 101 Squadron who, during June 1938, exchanged their aging Overstrands for the new monoplane bomber, the Blenheim. They initially received the Mk I but one year later, exchanged them for the Mk IV. This version had an increased range with improvements including armour plating, and under nose gun position and a twin-gun turret. The squadron worked up on the type at Bicester until 9th May 1939 when they moved to West Raynham in Norfolk.

The war came even closer with the Munich Crisis. As Mr Chamberlain flew to meet Adolf Hitler, Bicester in common with all military bases came to a state of full readiness. Buildings were hastily camouflaged, any white stone was painted black and personnel were told to carry arms at all times. This tense atmosphere was relieved a little when the PM arrived back at Heston with his 'little piece of paper'. It gave the country time but everyone suspected that it was only a breathing space.

During this period, two squadrons of Fairey Battles moved in from Andover as part of the force intended for France. Nos 12 and 142 Squadrons were among the first few squadrons to be selected as part of the Advanced Air Striking Force. They moved on to Berry-au-Bac the day before war was declared but even by this time, the type was hopelessly obsolete. On that same day, Neville Chamberlain sat with his colleagues in the House of Commons late into the night. They were still hoping that a letter from the German Chancellery would avert a war. They sat in agonizing silence, refusing to believe that Hitler would not reply and that peace would not prevail. As time wore on and no reply was forthcoming, Chamberlain rose and said quietly, 'Right gentlemen, this means war.' At 9 am the following morning the British

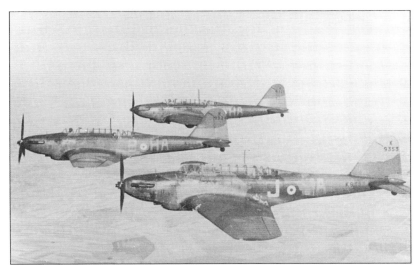

Fairey Battle bombers of No 218 Squadron. Like those stationed at the Oxfordshire airfields, these formed part of the Advanced Air Striking Force sent to France in 1939. (Crown via Air Britain)

Ambassador in Berlin handed Hitler a final note demanding a reply within two hours. No answer was received and at 11.15 am, the PM broadcast to the nation. The war had begun.

With the Battle squadrons in France, Nos 104 and 108 Squadrons brought their Avro Ansons to Bicester on 17th September 1939. Both converted to the Blenheim IV a month later and disbanded at Bicester on 6th April 1940 to form No 13 OTU. Training for Blenheim crews began immediately with a satellite airfield being established at Weston-on-the-Green. A decoy airfield was set up by Colonel Turner's Department at Grendon Underwood whilst further night flying was to be done at Hinton-in-the-Hedges. It was the beginning of Bicester's war and for one airman, Mr R. L. Barnard, the beginning of his war as well.

'I arrived at Bicester from St Athan around the 10th September 1939 and was posted to No 108 Squadron. I did my first flight in an Anson during a one hour formation flying sortie and later moved onto Blenheims. The winter of 1939 was one of the coldest and only occasionally did we bother to get the aircraft out of the hangar for running-up. Although I was not aircrew, I managed a fair bit of flying, sometimes in the gun turret but later on in the co-pilot's seat. The wireless operator/air gunners at this time were airmen but when the Air Ministry realised this, they were all rapidly promoted to Sergeants much to the disgust of the old sweats! However, any flight in a Blenheim was a risky business even with no part being played by Jerry so they deserved the promotion.

When Russia attacked Finland during the winter of 1939/40, many Blenheims appeared on the airfield for transit to Helsinki. The Finnish national emblem was a Swastika but the other way round. This was duly painted on the side of the Blenheims and whitewashed over for the journey. However, before departure, overnight rain removed the whitewash and gave rise to some stories in Bicester that many aircraft on Bicester airfield were captured German aircraft. I can still see the Finnish pilots in very heavy greatcoats and looking rather elderly, as I expect many were civil pilots.

Sadly, there were many crashes around the local area, some of which I photographed. Unfortunately, when the military police looked through my kit and found the camera, I found myself on a charge with the camera being confiscated. It was later returned to me minus the film. One of the crashes I saw was outside the airfield. Seeing the great cloud of smoke, I and several others ran towards it to see if we could help. The cockpit was an inferno and no hope for anyone. I sought refuge behind a haystack in case there was any ammo aboard only to find the two pilots casually smoking their cigarettes. How on earth they got out is anyone's guess but they were certainly lucky.'

In great secrecy, the prototype of the Handley Page Halifax had been assembled and test flown from Bicester on 25th October 1939. As November 1940 approached it heralded a change in tactics for the Luftwaffe. The county had suffered very little from the ravages of the Battle of Britain but watched with anguish the gathering storm that was to be called the Blitz. On the morning of Wednesday, 13th November 1940 however, the airfield could have been the subject of a forthcoming raid had the reconnaissance aircraft not been shot down.

This was a Ju 88 of LG1 (s/n 6157) that was detailed to carry out a surveillance of Oxfordshire. As it crossed the county, it overflew Bicester and was subjected to a volley of shots from the airfield defence Lewis guns which at that time claimed hits on the aircraft. As it passed into Berkshire, it was attacked by Flt Lt W. J. Leather and P/O Johnson in Spitfires of No 611 (West Lancashire) Squadron. With smoke coming from one engine, it made a forced landing at Woodway Farm, Blewbury in Berkshire. Fw W. Erwin, Uffz H. Wermuth and Fw E. Zins were taken prisoner but Gefr H. Bossdorf was found to be dead. The aircraft, L1/Ls although damaged, was later put on display in St Giles Street in Oxford amid great interest. (This incident is also covered in the Harwell chapter.)

No 13 OTU in its first year had trained 217 pilots, 240 observers and 273 air gunners. With the demand for Blenheim crews increasing all the time, the OTU was hard pushed to meet its commitments. The flying hours increased from 26,670 in the first year to 32,718 in the second, a considerable increase. Unlike the other bomber OTUs flying the Whitleys and Hampdens, the Blenheims were not engaged on 'Nickelling' operations so the amount of flying hours were purely used up by normal flying training.

From 1940 to 1941 and into 1942, nothing really happened to upset the normal practice of training although there were changes to the satellite airfields as Finmere and Turweston took their turns in acting as such. One significant episode however in the history of the unit and the airfield came when No 307 Ferry Training Unit formed at Bicester during 1942. This was in preparation for Operation 'Torch', the Allied landings in French North Africa planned for 8th November 1942. Whilst the operation had been in preparation for only three months, the conception went back to 1941. It was the first Allied experience of joint planning and operations including the British and American Chiefs-of-Staff. In the end however it turned out that the command structure for the landings was exclusively American.

No 13 OTU were tasked with the job of training crews to ferry replacement Blenheims urgently needed in Africa. Training commenced on the Blenheim V on 24th December 1942 for 30 crews with the final sortie being flown on 5th April 1943.

No 1551 Beam Approach Training Flight was formed at Bicester from the Beam Approach Calibration Flight which had disbanded on 29th November 1942. The unit came with four Ansons, three Oxfords and two Masters. By now these aircraft were conspicuous by their display of yellow triangles on the fuselage and wings. Usually a white, or sky or pale blue letter was applied alongside but a few units painted a black letter on the fuselage triangles.

With few German aircraft to worry about in the Oxfordshire area at this stage of the war, training continued unhindered with No 13 OTU. With many thoughts turning to the festive period, it was time for changes at Bicester. Though the Blenheim had been the mainstay of the OTU and will forever be associated with the station, the times were changing fast as the war was progressively carried back to Germany. This meant newer and better aircraft.

Part of the Lend/Lease Act with America, the first Douglas Bostons had been shipped to England in the summer of 1941 and were modified for use with No 2 Group as a Blenheim replacement. Around 780 Boston IIIs were delivered to the RAF, some of which ended up with No 13 OTU. Likewise the North American Mitchell was first used by the RAF in October 1942. Developed from the NA-40 attack bomber of 1938, the original B-25 Mitchell for the US Army made its maiden flight on 19th August 1940. Over 800 Mitchells were delivered to the RAF, again, some going to No 13 OTU. Being somewhat larger and heavier than the earlier Blenheims, most of these aircraft flew from the Bicester satellite airfields of Weston-on-the-Green and Hinton-in-the-Hedges which by now had hard runways. The remaining Blenheims were to remain at Bicester.

A change of command came about at the same time when No 13 OTU left Bomber Command and became part of No 70 Group, Fighter Command. This had become necessary in order to train crews for the new 2nd Tactical Air Force. Some of the Blenheims were given a new lease of life for training purposes before the OTU passed to No 9 Group on 1st November 1943. This continued until 25th February 1944 when all Blenheim flying ceased at Bicester. The bitter end came later in the year when No 13 OTU were moved over to Harwell in October 1944 leaving the station with no flying units at all.

Bicester now became a transit centre for the dispatch of equipment to the 2nd TAF on the Continent as well as serving as a motor transport depot. The HQ of No 40 Group (Maintenance Command) arrived during February 1947, staying until 1961. Maintenance units were also present at Bicester over this period including No 71, within whose ranks was the Historic Aircraft Flight, responsible for restoring the Avro Lancaster now resident in the RAF Museum at Hendon.

Flying returned during 1959 when the Chipmunks of the Oxford University Air Squadron moved in. They remained until 1975, after a light anti-aircraft wing was formed as part of the strategic reserve. The RAF Gliding and Soaring Association arrived during 1970 and today are still resident.

Bicester itself closed as an operational station on 31st March 1976 but was transferred to the Army sometime later. The magnificent 1930s airfield buildings are likely to become listed as being of Architectural and Historical Interest and will be preserved. The MOD clothing research unit uses them at the present time. Though never firing a shot in anger, the units and the station itself did much in the way of training thousands of aircrew. It was a very necessary job and one that Bicester did well.

6

BRIZE NORTON

Friday, 16th August 1940 dawned mainly fair and warm with a haze over the Channel. It heralded the advent of a lovely summer's day marred only by the fact that the country was at war. The plotting tables at Fighter Command at Stanmore in Middlesex were quiet, the Waafs sitting around the table slightly bored by the inactivity. This changed at 11 am, when a raid was plotted crossing the Channel and heading for the Home Counties. Again during the early part of the afternoon, a large raid materialised and headed for Southampton and Portsmouth causing a vast amount of damage.

After this the radar screens were quiet until late afternoon when a further enemy attack took place. As they crossed the East Coast, the formation, harassed by our fighter squadrons, broke up with two Ju 88s flying inland and finding Brize Norton.

Coming in low over the southern end of the airfield, they headed straight for the hangar complex and dropped 32 bombs. Their aim was very good with a direct hit on one of the hangars. It was a devastating blow with 32 Oxfords and 11 Hurricanes disintegrating in one huge explosion. One 250 kilo bomb landed close to the ammunition dump but fortunately failed to explode. The other bombs wrecked buildings with the result that ten casualties were taken to the sick bay. Surprisingly, there was no loss of life considering many of the personnel were out in the open either going to or coming from tea. In what seemed like minutes but was really only seconds, the enemy aircraft had climbed away and out of sight leaving behind the most destruction ever done to an Oxfordshire airfield.

It was the village of Clanfield that had originally been chosen for the site of an airfield in the 1930s. This low lying area was prone to flooding and so another site bounded by the villages of Brize Norton, Carterton and Black Bourton was found. It was decided to call the site

Brize Norton and by 1935, construction had begun on what was to be a sizeable airfield. Five 'C' Type hangars were to be included in the planning with a large domestic and technical site. Dispersed around the airfield perimeter were to be four further hangars.

Brize Norton officially opened on 13th August 1937, although far from completion, and No 2 FTS arrived from Digby on 7th September. They flew a mixture of the Hawker biplanes, Harts, Audaxes and Furies. The accommodation, after the relative comforts of Digby, came as quite a shock. Most of the personnel had to live in wooden huts which were heated by a central stove and proved very draughty.

Incorporated in the training schedule were detachments to armament practice camps. On one such occasion shortly after the unit arrived at Brize, an entire detachment was lost over Wales when it encountered bad weather. Even when the bombing range was changed

An aerial view of Brize Norton shortly after it opened in 1937. (RAF Brize Norton via Steve Bond)

to Dorset, several accidents resulted in loss of life, mainly due to weather problems.

On 10th October 1938, No 6 MU was formed at the airfield, occupying one of the hangars on the main site. They were to carry out the modification, storage and reissue of various types before returning them to the squadrons. Part of No 41 Group Maintenance Command, very many types were to pass through the unit. So much so that by the end of February 1939, over 200 aircraft had been received.

For No 2 FTS, the end of the Hawker biplanes was fast approaching. On 22nd February 1938, the first of the Airspeed Oxfords arrived. Several more came along in the following months accompanied by a few North American Harvards. The Station Flight was to receive a rather more unusual aircraft when a De Havilland Don was allocated to it. Originally designed to Specification T.6/36 as an advanced trainer with a dorsal turret, the order was cut from 250 to just 50 of which only 47 were built. In the end the dorsal turret was deleted for the RAF delivery but the life of the Don was very short, most of them being grounded by 1940.

It did, however, survive long enough to be displayed at the 1939 Empire Air Day held on Saturday, 20th May 1939. From early morning, crowds had been gathering at the airfield perimeter to watch the RAF at work. At this time they were not allowed onto the airfield, but they were not disappointed as the Oxfords, Harvards and the Don flew in mock combat with each other. Many suspected that this was to be the last air display of peacetime as the rumblings from Germany became ever more obvious.

As the rundown to war gathered pace, No 2 FTS were to face some changes. They were redesignated No 2 SFTS in September 1939 with the biplanes now withdrawn. The School would become an all Oxford unit in June 1940. At the same time, detachments of Nos 101 and 110 (Hyderabad) Squadrons brought their Bristol Blenheims in from West Raynham and Wattisham respectively, remaining for only one week during an exercise.

With more permanent accommodation now built, the task of camouflaging took priority. All the buildings and hangars were painted to merge into the background whilst white kerbstones and bollards were painted black and green. The landing area was painted to resemble several fields with hedges breaking them up thus making it difficult for the enemy to detect. Weston-on-the Green, Akeman Street, Witney and Southrop (in Gloucestershire) were designated as satellites,

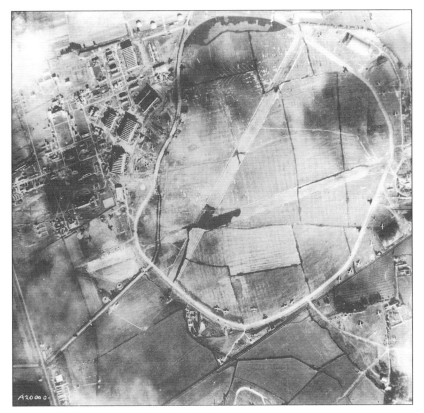

By 1943, the runways have been laid and the effect of camouflage is evident. (RAF Brize Norton via Steve Bond)

and a decoy airfield was built at nearby Chimney. A few days before the outbreak of war, B Company (Witney) of the 5th (TA) Oxfordshire and Buckinghamshire Light Infantry were called up to defend the airfield. Apart from a fortnight's camp, they had received no real military training and though dressed as soldiers, they had very little in the way of weapons. What they had were of World War One vintage. Rather like the Home Guard, they were allowed home when not on duty but many preferred to stay in the airfield mess where it was warmer and not full of evacuees! This was how Brize Norton went to war.

The onset however brought very little change to the training routine.

89

No 6 MU had the task of sending Gladiators to Finland and Blenheims to Yugoslavia in an effort to stem the progress of the war in that region. Like most of the country, Brize was in the grip of a very cold spell over the Christmas and New Year of 1939/40. Life became unbearable with frozen water pipes, lack of sufficient heating and the fact that all non-duty personnel were put to snow clearing.

By March things were getting back to normal. On 11th June 1940 part of No 15 SFTS moved in from Middle Wallop (see *Hampshire Airfields in the Second World War*), whilst awaiting a permanent move to Kidlington.

No 2 SFTS became the victim of an early tragedy on 28th July 1940. With the commencement of night flying training, many Oxfords on that night were airborne within the local area. Unknown to them was the fact that enemy aircraft were present within the county. It was not until an Oxford, crewed by Sgt Adkinson and Sgt Ward, was shot down over Akeman Street that it became apparent.

This may well have been a prelude to the 16th August raid which is chronicled at the start of the chapter. Some observers at the time said that the two German aircraft had joined the circuit with their wheels down as if to land, so avoiding detection. Whatever their method, the destruction was intense and certainly the loss of so many Oxfords to No 2 SFTS and the eleven Hurricanes of No 6 MU ensured that most of the other aircraft on Brize were quickly dispersed to the landing grounds at Southrop and Akeman Street.

There was no doubt that the enemy had made a mess of Brize Norton. The smoke from the burning hangar and its contents seemed to hang around for days despite the efforts of the fire crews, both military and civil. Mangled metal, wood and rubble lay everywhere with parts of aircraft still smouldering. Yet despite the intense damage, the airfield was only out of operation a short time. Once most of the damage had been cleared, it was back to the training routine. The remainder of 1940 and 1941 saw no further raids. There were sadly, however, many accidents due to the nature of the training with a considerable loss of life.

No 6 MU were still occupying another part of the airfield. With so many aircraft using their facility, the expansion of Brize became a necessity. This was not without its problems as the main Witney to Fairford railway line now crossed the airfield including cutting through one of the new taxiways for the aircraft. Undaunted, the military arranged to erect two large gates in the manner of a railway/aircraft

90

crossing. These were hastily built and camouflaged so as not to allow any enemy aircraft the chance to follow the railway line directly onto the airfield. Some enemy pilots used the rail system as a means of navigation by day, following the glow of the steam engines by night.

The MU were also not immune to tragic accidents. One of the worst was when an Anson that was engaged on ferrying pilots around the different airfields, crashed on the approach to Brize Norton. Tragically, all five on board were killed. Later on 22nd December 1940, a Hurricane crashed in a bad snow storm also with tragic results.

Despite these and other tragedies, one incident which could have proved fatal did have a humorous side to it. On 28th February 1941, a Spitfire which had received attention at No 6 MU was being tested by a Czech or Polish pilot. The usual practice when running up a single-engined aircraft on the ground was to have one or two people holding the tail down lest the slipstream from the propeller lifted it. On this particular occasion, one man was holding the tail down. This was unbeknown to the pilot who, when satisfied with the engine run, taxied and took off with the poor groundcrew man still hanging onto the tail. Realising what was wrong due to the handling of the aircraft, the pilot carefully turned back and landed safely with the man still clinging on. Full of apologies, the pilot leapt from the cockpit to find him none the worse for his flight. Apparently, the language used by the airman to the pilot was unprintable, but such happenings were very rare.

In addition to No 2 SFTS, Brize was now to become the home of No 1525 Beam Approach Training Flight. Arriving on 18th February 1942 with Oxfords, they stayed until 16th July 1942. In between this period, No 2 SFTS became No 2 (Pilot) Advanced Flying Unit, for pilots who had trained in the Dominions, such as Canada. They finally disbanded in July 1942. They had been at Brize to share the sorrows and triumphs of 1940 and 1941 but now the base was to enter a new training phase, that of heavy glider conversion.

The Airspeed Horsa glider was the RAF's first operational troop carrying glider. First flown in 1941, it was followed by a 3,655 production run. With a crew of two pilots, it was capable of carrying 20 to 25 troops. Of all wooden construction, it proved quick and easy to manufacture and became the workhorse of all the major Allied landings. When the new glider came into service in 1942, it became necessary to form a new unit in order to train army pilots to fly it. Accordingly, on 15th July 1942, the Heavy Glider Conversion Unit moved in to Brize Norton.

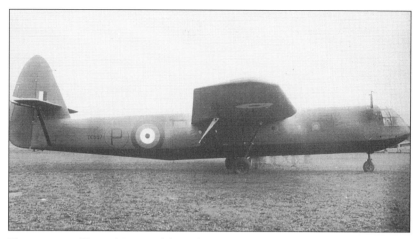

The prototype Airspeed Horsa glider. This was the main troop-carrying glider of the Second World War. (Crown)

With an initial complement of 50 Horsas, 34 Whitley Vs and two Oxfords to act as tugs, the training courses began. Throughout the rest of June and July, Horsas were being delivered from Airspeed enabling the figures at the end of July to stand at 307 day flights and 38 night flights.

It fell to No 6 MU to assemble the Horsas directly from the factory. With other types of aircraft that were also the responsibility of the MU, Brize was becoming very overcrowded. In order to ease the congestion, a new satellite airfield on the Duke of Bedford's estate at Woburn Abbey came into use in November 1942. Yet even with this new facility, it was found that further space was needed. Accordingly, some flying with the HGCU was transferred to nearby Grove airfield.

With the 16th August 1940 attack by the Luftwaffe still in mind, an additional decoy airfield was set up at Tadpole Bridge. Not functional during the day, come twilight a team from Brize Norton would cross to the decoy and lay a dummy runway with goose-neck flares.

Brize was still a very busy station even with the two additional landing sites. Accidents became more prevalent with the increased training, one which was particularly bad occurring on 9th November 1943. Two Whitleys involved on a night flying exercise decided to practise some low-level flying. Seeing what was happening, a third Whitley joined them resulting in a tragic crash between two of the

Waafs cheerfully give a hand pulling the heavy tow ropes towards the gliders. (Imperial War Musuem – ref. CH12797).

aircraft. One came down alongside the Witney Road whilst the other crashed onto some farmland. Four of the crew perished in the accident. On another occasion a Horsa glider crashed with the death of six people. Tragedy was never far away.

The Whitleys were labouring on when in early 1943 the first Armstrong Whitworth Albemarles came to Brize to act as tugs. Although built as a bomber, the Albemarle never served in that role, finally becoming a glider tug and special transport aircraft. Though they did arrive at Brize, they were not used in a flying role and were eventually sent back to the MUs in April 1943.

At the time no reason was given for their rapid departure, but it had been decided that the airfield was to lose the training role and become a major glider troop carrying base. The HGCU moved to North Luffenham during March 1944 and at the same time, Brize became part of No 38 Group. The airfield became home to Nos 296 and 297 Squadrons who brought their Albemarle IIs in from Hurn and Stoney Cross to train as glider tug squadrons. One hundred Horsas were allocated to the airfield and training began in earnest for D-Day.

Across the Channel, the preparations had begun to repel the expected invasion. A plan had been devised to fortify the coastline with underwater obstacles which would, according to Field Marshal Rommel, take a heavy toll of the landing craft before they hit the beach. To prevent airborne landings, fields and open areas within seven miles of the coast would be covered in heavy posts and anything that would hinder a glider landing safely. With these sort of obstructions, a glider packed with troops would have very little chance of survival. Luckily, the time allowed for such preparations was not sufficient to ensure that the invasion was beaten back.

Before this, the first major exercise for D-Day took place on 20th March 1944. Fourteen Albemarles from each squadron dropped paratroops onto Brize Norton before releasing their towed gliders. Deemed a success, it was followed by several others right up until the time of D-Day, 5th/6th June. Then, with a strong security cloak thrown around the airfield, the final briefings for the assault began.

Throughout Oxfordshire, troops were getting ready for the signal to go. Early evening on 5th June saw the airfield a hive of activity as the paratroops prepared to board the first 18 Albemarles. These were the

Troops embarking on a Horsa glider for a rehearsal drop. (Imperial War Museum – ref. CH10869)

94

Preparing for D-Day, a Whitley gets airborne towing a Horsa glider. (Imperial War Museum – ref. CH10341)

main body of the 5th Parachute Brigade who were to be dropped on landing zone 'N'. Their job was to prepare the landing zone for the Horsa gliders that were to follow. 'N' was a position six miles from the coast and six and a half miles north-east of Caen on the banks of the River Orne.

As midnight passed, the troops boarded the Albemarles and took off. At 03.20, the paratroops left the 18 aircraft, which turned and headed back to the airfield. At the same time the second wave of Albemarle tugs were hauling the Horsas into the air. Eight aircraft were from No 296 Squadron and nine from No 297 Squadron. Further tugs and gliders were also leaving Harwell and Tarrant Rushton.

With very few obstructions, the Horsas landed successfully. The job of the men was to capture two bridges over the River Orne and the Caen Canal. 'D' Company of the 2nd Battalion, The Oxfordshire and Buckinghamshire Light Infantry (52nd Light Infantry), were the first Allied unit to land in Normandy. They crossed the Channel from Brize in six Horsas, each carrying about 25 men. Once over their designated drop zone, the gliders were released with the usual twang. As the tugs turned to go back, the noise of their engines gradually faded to be replaced by total silence save for the sounds of the wind over the glider's wings as it headed down to land.

There to record the landing was a BBC correspondent: 'The paratroops are landing. They are landing all around me as I speak. They're coming from the sea, and they are fluttering down, red, white and blue parachutes fluttering down and they are just about the best thing we have seen for a good many hours. They're showering in, there is no other word for it. It's just about 9 o'clock and a whole mass of gliders has just come in having been towed across the Channel from Britain. They have received a particularly severe welcome from the German ack-ack defences and the flak has been going up from all around us. I can see four or five coming in, through the trees, skimming very low, over the ploughed fields and coming in to touch down. There will barely be room for them, so congested is the area with Allied gliders and troops.'

The landings proved bumpy as the gliders come down, lift up again and make a second contact with the ground. With the men inside being thrown around in their wooden seats, the only light comes from the

Ground crew checking and preparing a glider before a flight. (Imperial War Museum – ref. CH10361)

Horsa gliders landed at the Caen canal bridge, 6th June 1944. (Imperial War Museum – ref. MH2074)

sparks created by the glider's skids. One last touchdown and the Horsas push forward to bury their noses in the undergrowth or the bare earth. Suddenly all is silence. In seconds the troops realise they have to get out and smash their way through the broken exit. Almost at once they are met with a hail of bullets as they fall to the ground as one. No one is hurt but it is time to push forward and get to the bridge.

This they did, with the bridges being secured fairly quickly. Back at Brize Norton, the next phase was beginning as three Horsas towed by No 297 Squadron Albemarles crossed the Channel. Once over the French coast two successfully landed close to the coastal battery at Merville allowing the troops to capture it. The casement had appeared to be an impregnable fortress from aerial photographs taken earlier. Although the RAF had attempted to bomb it, the area was pock-marked with craters yet the battery itself was relatively untouched. Neither further bombing or shelling would obviously have an effect and so it was left to a glider borne force. The third glider broke its tow on the outward journey but managed to land safely at Odiham in Hampshire.

In the last operation of the day, code-named Operation 'Mallard', both squadrons managed to put up 20 Albemarles each to tow Horsas to another landing zone dispatching troops of the 6th Airborne Division. During the coming days and weeks, the Albemarles were used on supply dropping operations over the Allied lines as they pushed the enemy further and further back.

There was no respite for the squadrons as Operation 'Market', the code-name for the airborne operation at Arnhem, swung into action. For their role in this, the gliders were towed to Manston in Kent where the Albemarles were refuelled, allowing them maximum time over enemy territory. The 15th September saw the first of several sorties, some of the Albemarles towing Hadrian gliders in addition to the Horsas. On the 17th, a total force of 46 Horsas and 10 Hadrians were towed to Arnhem, joining many other squadrons employed on the same mission.

Operation 'Market Garden', the code-name for the ground advance,

Troops cover a Horsa glider with graffiti in 1944. (Imperial War Museum – ref. H39179)

was a humiliating failure and proved to be one of the big 'ifs' of the war. Historians place the blame on the air plan, devised by senior personnel, for the disaster to the airborne divisions. The landings were in daylight and the drop zones were too far from the objectives. The surprise to the enemy was lost earlier on, enabling the Germans to bring in strong reinforcements. Many considered Arnhem as the 'biggest cock-up of the war' and seeing what was happening on the ground saddened the aircrews of the Albemarles on their return to Brize Norton.

In the end, a grand total of at least 1,493 tug/glider combinations had been dispatched from the UK bases in the course of six operations. The part that the airfield had played in the final result cannot be overstated. It is a compliment to the ground and aircrews to record that throughout the campaigns, only one Albemarle was lost, when it crashed at Black Bourton killing seven personnel. Now, with the assault campaigns over, Nos 296 and 297 Squadrons moved to Earls Colne.

Brize Norton welcomed back the HGCU on 15th October 1944. Numbered No 21 HGCU, it returned with the now very aging Whitleys still employed on towing Horsas and Hadrians. Re-equipment to Albemarles did however take place during early 1945 when, with the scent of victory in the air, the training of RAF glider pilots ceased with training being given only to army personnel. With a surplus of aircraft available, experiments were conducted using differing types in the role of tugs. Stirlings and Halifaxes were now to be seen at the airfield but this was very shortlived as victory approached.

No 6 MU, throughout the Allied landings, had been continuing its sterling work. Though numerous types had passed through its doors during the early and middle part of the war, by 1944 it was mainly Spitfire work. The end of June 1944 recorded 301 aircraft in stock but as the end of the war approached, a most interesting change was about to take place.

The cessation of hostilities brought glider training at Brize to an end on 29th December 1945. No 21 HGCU moved to Elsham Wolds in Lincolnshire and the base was handed over to Transport Command with the School of Flight Efficiency and the Transport Command Development Unit moving in from Harwell. The interesting change was the resurgence of the Luftwaffe at Brize Norton, which must have brought back many unhappy memories. This time they even landed! Happy to report however, not to destroy the airfield, but to use it as a storage depot, for one of the aspects of the work of No 6 MU from August 1945 was the storage of captured German aircraft after their evaluation at Farnborough.

Among the first to arrive on 10th May 1945 was a Ju 88. This was followed by a Focke-Wulf 190, a He 219 and an Arado Ar 234 amongst many others. Sadly the vast majority of these were destined for the Brize Norton scrap heap on the south side of the airfield. With peace firmly established, this was the main job of the MU during 1945/46. Every type conceivable was cut up and sold for scrap. Today, of course, many of these types are having to be rebuilt from charred remains for the numerous air displays held yearly in the UK! Even the early Gloster Meteors fell to the axe before No 6 MU closed its doors on 31st December 1951.

Brize Norton in peacetime has seen a vast variety of aircraft passing through. From 1950 to 1965 it was used by the United States Air Force who flew both fighters and bombers from the base as part of the Strategic Air Command. On 1st April 1965, they had left and it returned to RAF control. Today it is an integral part of the RAF's strategic transport and tanker fleet and houses No 10 Squadron flying the BAC VC10, No 101 Squadron also with VC10s and No 216 Squadron flying the Lockheed Tristar. At this moment in time (February 2001), the early mark of VC10s are due to be phased out after a lifetime of valuable service. The remaining units are No 1 Parachute Training School, No 4624 (County of Oxford) Movements Squadron and No 2624 (County of Oxford) Squadron of the Royal Auxiliary Air Force. With the tendency of the government of the day to look to cost saving in the military, air to air refuelling and trooping movements, both of which are now carried out by the RAF from Brize Norton, may be sent out to private tender. However, the first of the RAF's new strategic transport aircraft, the Boeing C-17 Globemaster III was delivered to Brize Norton during May, and will bear the markings of newly reactivated No 99 Squadron. Perhaps therefore the future of this important wartime airfield is assured for many years to come.

7
BROADWELL

When D-Day finally came in the early hours of 6th June 1944, it proved to be the beginning of the end for the Third Reich. During 1943, the Americans had wanted the assault to be that year. The British, however, were concerned that the time had to be right and in the end, both allies came to an agreement that it should be June 1944. With their advance plans however, the Americans, in preparation, had devised a plan code-named 'Bolero' which called for American troops to be stationed in massive numbers in the UK ready for their intended invasion during 1943. It allowed for aircraft of the 8th Air Force to use twelve designated airfields in the UK, one of these being Broadwell. The plan was still open when it was agreed by both countries that the invasion should not take place until 1944 but by that time, Broadwell had already been allocated to RAF Transport Command who took control on 24th January 1944.

Situated three miles south of Burford and 340 feet above sea level, the airfield was not built until at least halfway through the war. When it was completed it took the typical three-runway bomber airfield layout. With the advance party arriving on 2nd February 1944 in order to prepare the new base for use, the Dakotas of Nos 512 and 575 Squadrons flew in from Hendon.

Committed to No 46 (Transport) Group, the Dakotas of both squadrons were delivered under the Lend/Lease Act. A total of 1,200 Dakotas were supplied to the RAF under the scheme, the type soon becoming the mainstay aircraft of Transport Command during this time. They were active as glider tugs, troop carriers, freighters and ambulances, all duties that were being carried out from Broadwell over this period.

April 1944 saw the airfield the scene of frantic activity as the first of several exercises leading up to D-Day took place. Exercise 'Dreme' called for a night landing of troops of the 1st Air Landing Brigade. Both Broadwell squadrons were involved with over 30 Dakotas taking part. As the Oxfordshire night air became heavy with the throb of Pratt and Whitney Wasp engines, the people of the county knew that a large assault on Europe could not be far away. The next exercise involved 35 Dakotas towing gliders and on 21st April, a full scale exercise codenamed 'Mush' involved 248 men jumping from 19 Dakotas.

Two days later, the Luftwaffe arrived over Broadwell. The records state that for the days of 22nd/23rd April, there was just one incident in East Anglia when 35 bombers crossed the coast between Portland Bill and Swanage. The enemy aircraft penetrated inland as far as Wiltshire and in the process, found Oxfordshire and Broadwell. Three HE bombs were dropped around the airfield perimeter with luckily, little damage being done. This was to be the first and the last time the Luftwaffe were seen in the sky above Broadwell.

As the run-up to D-Day continued, both squadrons were involved in leaflet dropping as part of the propaganda war. Further exercises took place until at the end of May, the station became sealed from the outside world amid strict security measures. This would continue until D-Day + 1 had dawned.

On the afternoon of 5th June, all the Dakotas were painted with black and white stripes on wings and fuselage to assist identification. With Operation 'Neptune', the code-name for the airborne forces commitment, fully implemented, the scene was set for the biggest invasion in

Practising for D-Day. Horsa gliders being towed by Halifax and Stirling tug aircraft. (Public Record Office)

history. Everything would depend on the safe and timely arrival of the invasion forces off the coast of Normandy. In the event, bad weather caused a postponement of 'Overlord' until the night of 5th/6th June but this postponement did have a good side for it lulled the Germans into thinking that an assault was not imminent, certainly not within two weeks! They had also become convinced that the invasion, when it came, would be just across the Channel along the Pas-de-Calais. This deception, the job of Operation 'Fortitude', had worked well and the element of surprise was still intact.

At Broadwell, over 1,000 troops were waiting for the signal to go. With a final briefing on the night of 5th June, the crews and troops tried to relax until it was time to lift off. The groundcrews had worked day and night preparing the aircraft for the operation, ensuring that there would be no problems. By 10 pm, the troops began boarding their respective aircraft and the signal to go was given to Wg Cdr Coventry of No 512 Squadron at 11.14 pm. Slowly at first, then gathering speed, his Dakota raced down the runway. In minutes it was airborne

A page of the Operations Records Book for Broadwell, showing the departure of Nos 512 and 575 Squadrons on D-Day. (Public Record Office)

followed by the rest of the squadron, 32 aircraft in all. Next it was the turn of No 575 Squadron led by Wg Cdr Jefferson. With the entire force airborne by 11.35 pm, they headed for the Channel coast and France.

Beneath them, the vast armada was heading in the same direction, on a somewhat more turbulent journey than the Dakotas. It was not long before the Normandy coast appeared and the paratroops began to make ready to drop. One by one, the Dakotas came in over the dropping zone, before turning back for Broadwell. As they did so, the British mainland was waking to the news that the invasion was on.

The BBC reporter, John Snagge, gave an authoritative account when he interrupted the normal schedules.

'This is the BBC Home Service. Here is a special bulletin read by John Snagge. D-Day has come. Early this morning the Allies began the assault on the north-west face of Hitler's European fortress. The first official news came just after 9.30 when Supreme Headquarters Allied Expeditionary Force, usually called SHAEF, issued communique No 1. This said, "Under the command of General Eisenhower, Allied naval forces supported by strong air

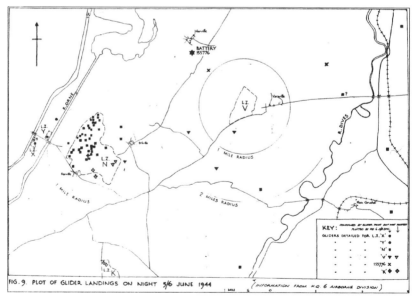

FIG. 9. PLOT OF GLIDER LANDINGS ON NIGHT 5/6 JUNE 1944

Plot of glider landings over the night of 5th/6th June 1944, the beginning of D-Day. (Public Record Office)

forces, began landing Allied armies this morning on the northern coast of France"'.'

By midday, the Dakotas of both squadrons were back at Broadwell. Once refuelled, the crews were briefed for another drop over the beachhead, this time towing Horsa gliders in daylight in an operation codenamed 'Mallard'. Eighteen aircraft from No 512 Squadron and 19 from No 575 Squadron were to be protected by a fighter screen for this operation, lest the Luftwaffe should put in an appearance. It turned out to be successful with good drops, the one exception being when one of the aircraft came down in the Channel with engine trouble. The initial landings and paratroop drops had come as a complete surprise to the Luftwaffe. No early reconnaissance aircraft had been in the air to report the advancing armada with the result that these first landings went fairly unhindered. It was only when, several hours into the operation, the enemy realised what was happening that the Luftwaffe was deployed over the landing area. By then the Broadwell squadrons had returned to carry out further drops.

Over the 7th and 8th June, the need arose for supplies to be dropped to the rapidly advancing Allied troops. Both squadrons participated in this for several days carrying food, water, ammunition and medical supplies.

On 17th June 1944, 15 Dakotas of No 575 Squadron left Broadwell for Holmsley South (see *Hampshire Airfields in the Second World War*), with 191 RAF men aboard. After refuelling, they left for France and landed at B5/Camilly airstrip, the first Dakota unit to land in France. Some moved on to B2/Bazenville airstrip, there to embark 254 casualties and fly them back to England. The rest of June, July and August followed a similar pattern with Dakotas bringing the wounded back to England. As September arrived, Broadwell entered another very hectic stage as Operation 'Market Garden' swung into action.

The plan was to capture the bridges over the lower Rhine in Holland. Once this was accomplished, Montgomery intended to advance east towards Osnabruck, Munster and Hamm and from here along the eastern face of the Ruhr. It was also planned that the Canadian First Army would clear the Scheldt Estuary in order for Antwerp to open as the main supply base for the Allied armies. This ambitious project was to involve the dispatch of the British 1st and American 82nd and 101st Airborne Divisions together with the 1st Allied Airborne Corps Headquarters. As history records, the operation failed in its aims due partly to bad weather, a shortage of tug aircraft, and the fact that the landing areas were about eight miles from their objectives.

Once again, two days before the planned commencement of 'Market Garden', Broadwell was subject to a big security clampdown. On 17th September, the date set for the invasion, 22 Dakotas of No 512 Squadron and 24 of No 575 Squadron left the airfield towing Horsa gliders. After a successful crossing, the aircraft arrived over the designated drop area, the gliders releasing as planned, only to find very poor visibility. This, added to the fact that the drops were nowhere near the correct zone, caused the operation to become a catastrophe. For the Broadwell squadrons, the losses of five gliders which released far too soon and of a glider pilot killed by enemy machine-gun fire near Oustahouet, were felt deeply by the Dakota crews.

The airlift, however, had to go on with the next sortie consisting of 41 gliders carrying 544 troops of the 1st Border Regiment, No 1 Airborne Division. In addition, the load contained jeeps, trailors, motor and ordinary cycles, hand carts and anti-tank guns. Once dropped, all the Dakotas returned safely to Broadwell.

Further sorties were flown to re-supply the troops, an incident on 18th September bringing home to all the crews just how dangerous these operations could be. On this particular day, 24 Dakotas were on the sortie. Flying over Turnhout, the AA guns below claimed the life of F/O Henry. In the same burst, the navigator was badly wounded and the aircraft itself damaged. The co-pilot, W/O Smith, took over control and turned back to England with the glider still in tow. With good forethought, the glider pilot released the tow thus allowing Smith more of a chance to reach England safely. This he did, landing at Martlesham Heath in Suffolk. In the same sortie, one of 575 Squadron's Dakotas was involved in another incident making it difficult to fly, whilst another Dakota of 512 Squadron was sadly lost.

The next day, 30 Dakotas left Broadwell for further supply drops, sadly both squadrons losing an aircraft due to a heavy concentration of flak within the dropping area. The next few days were spent in similar vein, so desperate was the need as the troops still struggled below to make headway. In order to be nearer the drop zones, 18 aircraft of 575 Squadron left Broadwell for B56 Brussels/Evere airfield. Still both squadrons carried out the arduous job of dropping food and supplies, until the end of the Arnhem operation.

With this, the repatriation of the wounded troops became a priority

One of the main Arnhem landing areas showing a scattering of gliders. (Public Record Office)

With the photographs brought back from Benson-based squadrons, rubber models were made up of the D-Day landing areas – 340 such models were sent out to commanders. (Imperial War Museum – ref. CH16106)

whilst Operation 'Varsity' entailed the Dakotas moving to Gosfield before returning to Broadwell on 25th March 1945. Still giving sterling service, the Dakotas of both squadrons continued the dropping of supplies and the repatriation of wounded up to and including the months after the German surrender on 6th May 1945.

On 6th August, both squadrons left Broadwell with No 512 moving to Holme-on-Spalding Moor and 575 to Melbourn. It had been a fairly short but very hectic time for them and a job very well done. No sooner had they left than further Dakotas arrived belonging to Nos 10 and 76 Squadrons. They were re-equipping for a move to the Far East, departing on 28th August 1945 to be replaced by No 77 Squadron which followed a similar pattern and had left for the Far East by 20th September. Although the war had ended in Europe, the Japanese were still the enemy.

It was not until 5th October 1945 that a new squadron of Dakotas was based at Broadwell. No 271 Squadron flew in from Odiham with Dakota IIIs and continued the duties within Transport Command

The Douglas C-47, or Dakota as the RAF called it. This example is part of No 320 Squadron but many similar served at Broadwell. (via A. Moor)

including the busy trunk route to India. On 1st December 1946, the squadron disbanded but was immediately reformed as No 77 Squadron and moved to Manston in Kent on 17th December. It was also the end of the long association with the Dakota for Broadwell.

Despite the fact that the airfield offered good runways and good accommodation, it was not required for peacetime use. With the departure of No 271 Squadron, the rundown to closure began, this finally taking place on 31st March 1947 when the RAF Ensign was lowered for the last time and RAF Broadwell passed into history. For many years after its closure the airfield lingered on but slowly time has taken its toll, much of the site finally being demolished. Though active for only a short period, Broadwell's contribution to the invasion and beyond was immense.

8
CHALGROVE

The Second World War accelerated aviation knowledge to an unprecedented degree. The advent of the jet-powered aircraft in 1944 brought with it numerous problems. Not only was it not known what effect very high speed would have upon a human body but with these higher speeds, the conventional way of leaving a military aircraft in trouble was impossible. The parachute for fast jet aircraft pilots was now redundant, a new method of safe escape had to be found. The solving of this problem would take place partly at Chalgrove.

Captured German records showed that they had made incredible progress in every sphere of aviation. In rocket-powered aircraft as well as jet-powered aircraft, they led the world at the end of the war. They too were researching the problems of escape from fast aircraft and were certainly ahead of Britain and the USA in this field of work.

The Gloster Meteor was the first jet aircraft to go into service with the RAF. It was also the only Allied jet to see action in the Second World War with the first one, DG206, flying on 5th March 1943. From that time on, it went through various stages of development and improvement until the first Mk 1s were delivered to No 616 (South Yorkshire) Squadron of the RAuxAF on 12th July 1944. It was however the Mk 3 that formed the equipment of Fighter Command's first post-war jet fighter wing when Nos 56 (Punjab), 74 (Trinidad) and 245 (Northern Rhodesia) Squadrons received them at Bentwaters. The final fighter mark was the F-8 which had a new concept in escape fitted. It was known as the ejector seat.

For some years, Martin-Baker had been engaged in research into escape from the new generation of jet aircraft. Whilst the work had begun during the war, it was the post-war period that saw the most development. The company had developed the idea of sitting the pilot

Work now carried out at Chalgrove by Martin Baker involves live ejections from the company Meteor. (Martin Baker)

in a seat that would enable him, by pulling a visor over his head, to be automatically fired out of the aircraft. The seat and pilot would separate, each one falling back to earth by parachute which would automatically deploy once clear of the aircraft.

The first test firing was done at Chalgrove on 24th July 1946 when Mr Bernard Lynch, a volunteer and an employee of Martin-Baker, was successfully ejected from the back seat of a specially converted Gloster Meteor flying at 320 knots at a height of 8,600 feet. From that one live ejection came the very sophisticated ejector seats that are fitted to today's supersonic aircraft. This fact alone placed Chalgrove in the history books.

Chalgrove was one of the Oxfordshire airfields that was not in use at the beginning of the war. In fact it was not deemed ready for occupation until late 1943 and even then it was unfinished. It was situated in a wide flat area that had seen the Battle of Chalgrove Field fought in June 1643. An obelisk a half mile from the village marked the

The moment of ejection. (Martin Baker)

battle and it was this area that was chosen to construct the airfield. It was not a pretty sight with the mud churned up by the construction gangs clinging to the boots of the men of the Headquarters, No 70 Group who had arrived to survey the site.

They found an airfield with three runways, 6,000 feet, 4,200 feet and again 4,200 feet, together with two T.2 hangars dispersed around the perimeter. There were 50 loops for aircraft dispersal and utility buildings for up to 2,368 people. Coming under the control of nearby Benson, Sqn Ldr H. A. Mockton had been appointed the first CO of Chalgrove. Surveying the state his airfield was in, he wondered what he had done to deserve such a posting!

What he did not know at this stage however, was that Chalgrove had been earmarked for the American 8th Air Force on 11th November 1942 as a transport or observation unit base. In December 1943, Colonel F. M. Paul of the US Service Command arrived to make preparations for the first American servicemen to arrive. Several days later a C-47 transport aircraft touched down with the first of the troops to occupy the base. At this point a change of allocation took place and Chalgrove became a base of the 9th Air Force. Command was handed over to Lt Col E. Haight on 6th January 1944 as around 1,000 airmen arrived.

For the locals it was a culture shock. Chalgrove after all was just a little village with a stream flowing each side, a picture of rural Oxfordshire. The sudden influx of so many Americans was bound to have an effect on village life although many of the locals did open their doors and offer some of them hospitality. For the Americans it was not that bad after all.

Before any American aircraft flew into Chalgrove, it was used briefly for the testing of model gliders. Produced by the world famous International Models company, responsible for the lovely 'Frog Penguin' models, they were needed as targets for air firing practise. Arriving from nearby Thame, the gliders were towed by a Defiant and a Martinet and proved such a success that International Models produced the targets for wartime and post-war service.

For several weeks after the new year, the men were busy preparing the base for the arrival of a squadron. On 27th January 1944, the 30th Photo Reconnaissance Squadron of the USAAF arrived and Chalgrove became officially operational. The arrival of the Lockheed P-38 Lightning at the base was a further shock to the locals. This long-range fighter and fighter-bomber had been converted to a PR version with cameras replacing the nose guns. Powered by two 1,475 hp

113

Allison V-1710-111/113 engines, its distinctive twin-boom layout gave it a maximum speed of 414 mph with a range of 2,260 miles. A rather noisy aircraft, it did not endear itself to the villagers of Chalgrove. The official handover to the USAAF from the RAF took place one windy day in February 1944 when the RAF Ensign was lowered to be replaced by the Stars and Stripes. Chalgrove was now known as USAAF Station No 465.

The 30th PR Squadron became part of the 10th Photographic Group on 21st February 1944. With plans well ahead for an Allied landing on the coast of Europe that year, a variety of PR tasks were carried out by the unit. Many low level photos were taken of enemy airfields and coastal defences surrounding the planned area of landing. Further help in photographing the entire coast came when the 31st, 33rd and 34th PR Squadrons joined the 30th Group. Their combined efforts resulted in the award of a Distinguished Unit Citation for all the units.

The Lightnings were often to be seen in the company of other aircraft such as the Martin B-26 Marauder. This aircraft was sometimes known as the 'widow maker', one of the most unpleasant names bestowed upon it. It did have its faults and problems but as a bomber and reconnaissance platform, it served its purpose well. Day after day these aircraft were over the enemy positions, bringing back the photos that were needed for the invasion, planned for 6th June 1944. A BBC broadcast by Frank Gillard captures very well the atmosphere of the period at Chalgrove and many other bases as well.

'England has become one vast ordnance dump and field park. In every wood and copse, in leafy dead end lanes and side roads, often in private gardens, under quarries and embankments, there it all was. Trucks, ambulances, tanks, armoured cars, carriers, jeeps, bulldozers, ducks. Vehicles of all kinds. Vast, really vast numbers of them. And right in the midst of it all, just as I turned for home, I passed a field where 22 men in khaki shirts and battle-dress trousers and heavy hob-nail boots, were having a quiet knock-up game of cricket. They made me think of Francis Drake and Plymouth Hoe as they prepared to go into battle.'

In the early hours of 6th June 1944, the invasion began. The assault was led by three airborne divisions followed by five assault divisions with tanks landing on the beaches, followed by another six with 21 more waiting in England. The question of timing was crucial for the

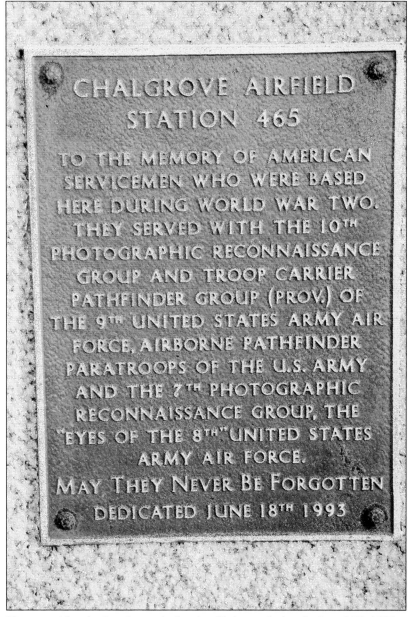

The memorial to the American units based at Chalgrove during the Second World War.

first wave of five divisions had to be pushing inland before the six that were to follow could be put ashore. Though fierce opposition was met and many lives were lost, by 12th June Montgomery had 326,000 men on French soil. As soon as the landings had been accomplished, the 10th PR Group began a hectic period photographing enemy troop positions, airfields and anything that could prove a hazard to the Allies moving rapidly inland. For two weeks after D-Day, the pressure was intense.

On 27th June 1944, the 15th Tactical Reconnaissance Group was transferred to the 10th from the 67th Tactical Reconnaissance Group bringing its P-51 Mustangs and F-6s to Chalgrove. At the same time, the 30th PR Squadron moved over to Middle Wallop, followed a month later by the 10th who, with the advancing Allies, moved to an airfield in France.

From this time until March 1945, Chalgrove assumed a more minor role. The hectic past few months had seen so many sorties mounted from the base that when the Lightnings and Mustangs had gone, an unreal silence pervaded the area. The closing days of the war saw the 7th PR Group deploy from Mount Farm to Chalgrove together with the P-51s and F-6s of the 22nd PR Squadron. It was still a very busy time

The remaining T2 hangar at Chalgrove now houses the company Meteor aircraft.

116

for the Americans for their expertise was needed for the purpose of evaluating by photographs the damage done to the countries that were occupied. This continued until December 1945 when the Group HQ finally left Chalgrove.

Once again the station came under the control of nearby Benson. By 1946 Martin-Baker had approached the military with a view to leasing Chalgrove in order to carry out tests with their ejector seats. As we have seen in the opening of the chapter, they were successful and today, continue to use Chalgrove though on a much smaller scale. From that short but very hectic period in its usage, one T2 hangar remains whilst the perimeter track and runway are still kept to usable condition and yes, the local villagers still talk about the time when the Americans came!

9
EDGEHILL

It is not generally known that ideas for a jet-powered aircraft were around in the 18th century! Nothing much came of it however, until the 1930s when, with flight firmly established, the need arose for more power than a piston engine with propellers could produce.

This later inspiration for a jet engine came from two Britons, Dr A. A. Griffiths of the Royal Aircraft Establishment at Farnborough and a young Cranwell officer, Frank Whittle. It was the latter that had first suggested the use of jet propulsion for aircraft back in 1929 but it was Griffiths who had carried out both theoretical and practical work three years earlier. The running of an axial compressor took place in 1936, the results of which encouraged an engineering company, Metropolitan-Vickers, to become involved in 1937.

The first jet engine to be designed by Whittle was tested the same year and such was the rate of progress that it was placed into a British designed aircraft and first flown in May 1941 in the Gloster E28/39. Whilst the initial flight trials and testing were done at Cranwell, it was at Edgehill that the later trials took place thus ensuring the airfield a permanent place in the story of British jet engine development.

Originally opened as a satellite to Moreton-in-the-Marsh in Gloucestershire on 21st October 1941, Edgehill was situated nine miles west-northwest of Banbury. Its first use was for the Wellingtons of No 21 OTU who were based at Moreton. Designed to a bomber airfield layout, Edgehill had three grass runways, one 1,600 yards long and two 1,200 yards long. No 21 was engaged in training new aircrew and leaflet drops, code-named 'Nickel', over Occupied Europe.

To return to the jet engine, forming a company called Power Jets Ltd in March 1936 had enabled Frank Whittle to continue his work with the utmost urgency. An amalgamation with Rover Cars, who were to build parts for the engine, ensured that taxiing trials were ready to begin on

7th April 1941. Powered by an 869 lb thrust Whittle W.1X turbojet and flown by R. E. G. Sayer, Gloster's Chief Test Pilot, the trials at Gloster's airfield were successful. Indeed, on one of the last tests, the aircraft actually became airborne for about 200 yards but no further trials were done at this time until the more powerful engine, the W1, was fitted.

By 15th May 1941, the E28/39 was ready once again for flight trials. After several high speed taxiing runs during the day, it was early evening when Frank Whittle was able to record simply: 'Evening – first test flight of the E28'. History had been made. With this, the aircraft was partially dismantled and moved to Cranwell for further testing. During its time there, the aircraft achieved 370 mph in level flight at 25,000 feet, well above the then top speed of the Spitfire. Its time at Cranwell gave rise to incredulity amongst Whittle's fellow officers. When one asked, 'How the hell does that thing work?', the other was heard to reply, 'Oh, it's easy old boy. It just sucks itself along like a Hoover!' On another occasion an officer was heard to comment: 'My God chaps, I must be going round the bend – it hadn't got a propeller!'

At this time, Rolls-Royce took an interest in Frank Whittle's work and were to continue to do so into the future. The aircraft, now named Pioneer W4041, continued its trials at Cranwell but when it came to an

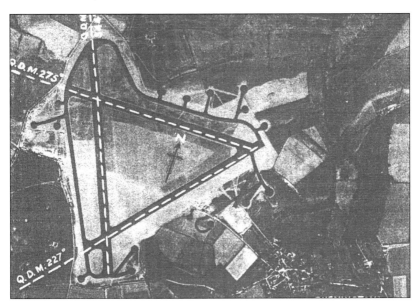

Wartime plan of Edgehill. (Public Record Office)

119

engine change, it was decided to carry out further trials at Edgehill. The removal of all the equipment from Cranwell to Edgehill took some time but flight trials began at the airfield during February 1942, the aircraft being flown as before by Gerry Sayer. Amidst tight security, taxiing trials began on 4th February 1942 and proved successful. A blade failure in March brought a temporary halt to further trials but speeds of 330 mph were reached at a height of 15,000 feet.

In April 1942, Rover's had completed building eight W2B engines but Power Jets were reluctant to install one of them directly into the aircraft and it was hoped to test the engine in a Wellington Test Bed. There were several Wellingtons at Edgehill around this time belonging to 21 OTU but when permission for the plan was given, the testing was actually done by Rolls-Royce in a Wellington based at their home airfield at Hucknall.

For No 21 OTU, meanwhile, as with the rest of the OTUs, tragedy was never far away, as an incident on 24th October 1941 and another on Sunday, 7th December serve to illustrate. In the first instance, a Wellington IC of 'B' Flight was carrying out a training exercise when it stalled at 400 feet. Despite gallant efforts by the pilot, Sgt Thackwall, the aircraft crashed at Lower Brailes, Warwickshire. In the ensuing fire which totally destroyed the Wellington, sadly only the rear gunner survived.

Sunday, 7th December 1941 was also a sad day for Edgehill when Wellington IC, s/n Z1089, encountered a heavy snow storm whilst on a training flight. Losing height and engulfed in low cloud, the aircraft struck the top of a telegraph pole on Pitch Hill near the villages of Sibford Gower and Swalcliffe. Two RAF officers seeing the stricken Wellington crash, rushed to help but were beaten back by the exploding fuel. Through the inferno they saw one of the crew attempting to get out of the aircraft and despite several attempts that ended in failure, with the help of the local policeman, they managed to drag the airman from the fuselage. To the amazement of the three men, a further crew member was found in a field beside the crash. However, out of a crew of six, Sgt R. Newton and Sgt J. Martin were the only survivors.

No 21 OTU crews were soon carrying out the first of a series of bombing raids over Germany. Having progressed from the 'Nickelling' leaflet raids, they were dispatched to Cologne in May 1942 followed by Essen and Bremen.

The hot summer of 1942 also allowed the continuation of the Gloster

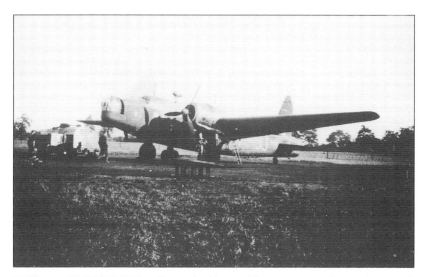

Wellington IC X9637 SJ-V at dispersal with petrol bowser in attendance. This aircraft was lost on 1st July 1942 when it crashed into the sea off Fowey, Cornwall on a cross-country training exercise. (Sqn Ldr R. R. Glass via Eric Kaye)

E28/39 test flights. Still in the capable hands of Gerry Sayer, the aircraft was demonstrated to many military personnel including Americans. Sadly, two days after the aircraft had been shown to the American military, Gerry was lost whilst flying a Typhoon. No definite conclusion was reached as to what happened but it was assumed that he had collided with another aircraft. The incident shocked all those who were connected with the trials, especially Frank Whittle. It fell to Michael Daunt to replace him but it was several months before trials began again.

In February 1943, the second Gloster E28/39, W4046, was taken to Edgehill for trials. Powered by the W2B engine built by Rover and flown by John Grierson, it reached speeds in excess of the previous aircraft at just over 400 mph. One memorable flight was made on 17th April when Grierson flew W4046 from Edgehill to Hatfield and demonstrated it to Winston Churchill. However, the trials at Edgehill were numbered and by late autumn, W4041 had been taken to Farnborough for further engine trials.

Edgehill was now in for another change when No 12 OTU from Chipping Warden took over the airfield as a satellite from No 21 OTU.

Three unidentified ground crew at dispersal with Wellington IC X9880 SJ-K. This aircraft took part in the 1,000 bomber raids on Cologne (pilot Sgt Williams) and Essen (pilot Flt Lt Hartford). (Eric Kaye Collection)

Two flights of the new unit arrived from Turweston on 27th April 1943 flying Wellington IIIs. This mark had become the main version in Bomber Command service with a total of 1,519 being built. Although the aircraft had a top speed of 255 mph and a range of 2,200 miles with 1,500 lb of bombs, it was replaced by the Wellington X in August. In addition to the Wellingtons, the OTU Target Tow and Gunnery Flight arrived with Hurricane IIs and Martinet Is. The latter were used for towing the target drogues whilst the Hurricanes were used for carrying out simulated attacks on the Wellingtons which allowed the gunners using camera guns to register hits on the fighter.

Despite a hard winter during 1944, training continued unabated with the usual crop of incidents concerning the novice crews. The night of 10th December 1944 must rank among the more unusual, as related by Sgt Alec Pennock and recalled here from the book, *The Story of RAF Edgehill* with permission from its author, Eric G. Kaye.

'Allocated Wellington Mk III BK131, pupil pilot Flt Sgt Reg Edwards and crew were detailed to fly a night sortie on fighter

122

affiliation. All pre-flight checks having been completed, the Wellington took off to rendezvous with the Hurricane fighter. While still trying to locate the fighter, a radio message ordered a change of detail to that of carrying out 'circuits and bumps'.

Joining the circuit as another aircraft took off, Flt Sgt Edwards followed the Drem runway lights into the approach funnel and onto the runway when he was conscious of something flashing through the beam of the aircraft landing light. In the next few seconds there was an almighty bump and the bomber bounced across the runway with sparks and debris in its wake. It then bounced and slid halfway across the airfield before finally coming to a halt. Within seconds, Sgt Pennock was out of the astrodome hatch hastily followed by the other members of the crew.

Leaving BK131 with serious damage to the port engine, propeller and undercarriage, the crew climbed onto one of the rescue tenders for a ride to the control tower to face the officer in charge of flying. After he had heard Sgt Pennock's explanation on what he thought may have been the reason for the mishap, the officer gave them all a disbelieving look and ordered them to sick

Watch office (control tower) and adjacent buildings. The framework on top of the tower is the frame to receive the numbers board for the operational runway. Photograph taken on a snowy winter's day 1987. (Eric Kaye Collection)

quarters for the customary medical checks, but requesting their return after medical clearance.

Returning to flying control after being given the all clear from the MO, Flt Sgt Edwards was told that there had been something on the runway and that he hadn't been seeing things. In fact, what his aircraft had hit was a cow! The animal had wandered on the runway after getting through a defective fence.'

After the excitement of the Gloster jet trials, life must have seemed fairly tame at Edgehill. Although not directly taking any part in the D-Day landings on 6th June 1944, the arrival of a P-38 Lightning on that day was something of an occasion. The aircraft was based at nearby Chalgrove with the 10th Photographic Group of the USAAF and had put down at Edgehill with an overheating engine. Together with a B-17 Fortress that had landed sometime previously after returning from Germany and not being able to make its home base, the atmosphere was definitely American around that significant time. Even more

The RAF memorial stone dedicated on Sunday, 8th September 1991, 50 years to the day after personnel from No 21 OTU Moreton-in-Marsh moved in to open up the airfield. The service was conducted by Lord Stuart Blanch, the former Archbishop of York. (Eric Kaye Collection)

exciting was the departure of the B-17 when it used the entire length of the Edgehill runway and was in fear of overshooting. With cheers and hand clapping from the Edgehill personnel, it managed to get airborne with just feet to spare.

The OTUs continued their fine work until June 1945 but with reduced flying by No 12 OTU, movements mainly consisted of diverted aircraft either caused by bad weather or engine problems. When the OTU closed, Edgehill was used as a storage site by No 25 Maintenance Unit but by the end of 1949 it had been placed under Care and Maintenance.

It saw a brief resurgence of use in 1953 when it became a temporary satellite for No 1 Flying Training School at Moreton-in-the-Marsh. The Korean crisis brought the sound of aircraft back to Edgehill with Harvards and Percival Prentices using its facilities. The final end came in 1954 when the Ensign was lowered for the last time and no further use was made of RAF Edgehill. Today there are still signs of its existence, a site that contributed much to the advent of the modern military jets such as the Tornado and Jaguar as well as the training of many of the Bomber Command aircrew.

10
HARWELL

On Tuesday, 28th September 1944, the headlines in the *Daily Mail* told of an epic that, whilst a failure in many people's eyes, would go down in history as one of the bravest of operations.
The report read:

> Two thousand troops of the First British Airborne Division were evacuated from the Arnhem bridgehead out of 7,000 to 8,000 dropped in the area, according to the American broadcast from Paris last night.
> About 1,200 wounded were left behind in the care of the Germans and the British doctors who stayed with them. The Germans claimed that they held 6,150 prisoners, including 1,700 wounded and that British killed numbered 1,500.
> At SHAEF last night it was emphasised that the Arnhem operation must not be regarded as a failure. Without it we could never have hoped to capture the even more vital Nijmegen bridge where the Waal is twice as wide as the Lower Rhine at Arnhem. Two or three days is regarded as the fighting span of airborne troops. The First Division held out for nine days. Bad weather eventually made withdrawal necessary.

One of the airfields closely associated with the Arnhem Operation was Harwell and it was from here that Short Stirling bombers towed Horsa gliders to the drop zone. Nowhere else in the county was the failure of Operation 'Market' felt so deeply. It did, however, add another chapter to the remarkable history of this airfield.
Used in the beginning as a temporary night landing ground, Harwell

126

came to the attention of the Works Directorate when it was decided to build a bomber airfield on the original site. It first came under RAF control in February 1937 and in April, No 226 Squadron flew their Hawker Audaxes in from Upper Heyford. They were joined by No 105 Squadron on 26th April 1937 with the same type together with the Hawker Hinds of No 107 Squadron who came in from Old Sarum on 15th June 1937.

Though classed as bomber squadrons, there was at this time a shortage of large bomber aircraft and so the Army Co-operation Audax and biplane Hind were just a stop-gap. With the Fairey Battle single-engined bomber reaching the squadrons, No 105 were the first to convert followed by No 226 Squadron.

Training for the eventual war began immediately and in September 1939, they would all join to form No 72 Wing and leave for France in an attempt to help stem the German advances. Before they left, however, Harwell hosted the last Empire Air Day of peace in May 1939. Thousands turned up to watch the vastly expanded air force at work. At this time aircraft types on display were guarded by armed military guards and the mock dog-fighting and bombing displays were more than a little realistic. One aircraft on static display was the Bristol Blenheim, the first of the monoplane twin-engined bombers. The year before, No 107 Squadron had received the Blenheim but by the Empire Air Day, they had moved to Wattisham.

With the declaration of war in September 1939, No 75 (New Zealand) Squadron flew their Wellington Is in from Stradishall. Immediately, detachments were sent to Squires Gate, Carew Cheriton and Honington. No 75 Squadron were preceded by No 148 flying Ansons and with the setting up of a 'Q' site decoy at Beedon, Harwell prepared to go to war.

The winter of 1939/40 was certainly one of the cruellest on record with much of the country deep in snow and frost. Harwell was no exception with water pipes continually frozen, lack of heating fuel and the hands-on job of endeavouring to keep the aircraft ice free. The weather restricted flying for much of January and February but with the better weather coming in March, the Wellington Is were exchanged for the IA mark.

On 4th April 1940, 75 and 148 Squadrons amalgamated to become No 15 OTU with a complement of both Wellingtons and Ansons. With this, training for pilots began immediately with the first operational flight over enemy territory taking place on the night of 18th/19th July

An example of the leaflets dropped on 'Nickelling' operations.

1940. This involved a 'Nickelling' operation for three Wellingtons who dropped leaflets over the French coast. Later in the month further 'Nickelling' was carried out, every sortie proving successful and thoroughly good training for the crews and trainee pilots. At the same time, 20 Whitleys were detached to Harwell to carry out several raids on Milan. They had flown in from Dishforth to refuel and arm before making the long trip to Italy and back.

Along the south coast, the Battle of Britain was intensifying with August seeing the greatest threat. Friday the 16th was a typical sunny summer day with just the amount of haze the Luftwaffe liked to carry out surprise attacks. The radar stations noted no appreciable build-up of enemy aircraft until after midday when they notified Stanmore of three heavy raids coming over the Channel. In all they noted about 350 aircraft approaching, spread out the length and breadth of the south and east coasts. Some came inland to bomb East Anglia and at around 6 pm, a lone aircraft appeared over Harwell and dropped four bombs.

With one huge explosion, two petrol bowsers caught fire throwing burning fuel and pieces of metal high into the air. Three Wellingtons were destroyed in the inferno, and sadly two airmen were killed and five badly injured when the enemy turned his machine guns on the airfield. In seconds, which must have seemed far longer, silence returned except for the crackling of many fires. With darkness approaching, only a little clearance could be carried out. This may have been fortuitous for around midnight, Harwell was again subjected to an attack, this causing only slight damage. The two raids, however, convinced the Air Ministry that Harwell could be the target for further major attacks and consequently, the aircraft were dispersed to another satellite airfield at Hampstead Norreys.

Yet again, on Monday, 19th August 1940 another three Wellingtons were destroyed after a bombing and strafing attack by a single Ju 88. Clearance from the previous raid was on-going at the time and once again, fire and explosions devastated Harwell. All station personnel including trainees at No 15 OTU were put to clearing the rubble to ensure the airfield could once again operate. There was no respite however, as on Monday, 26th August, the Luftwaffe returned and again bombed Harwell. Though not as severe as the previous raids in damage, sadly six RAF personnel and ten civilians were badly injured. August had proved a bad month for Harwell as for some reason, the German Intelligence believed it to be a bomber airfield.

Whilst the Battle of Britain was still raging in the south of the country, No 15 OTU carried on with its training routine. Further 'Nickelling' was carried out during September accompanied by the ever present accidents. Another problem for the trainee crews was the balloon cables that stretched across various parts of the land and the risk of flying into them. Such an incident happened on 18th September 1940 when a Wellington of the OTU flew into a cable, though escaping severe damage and managing to land safely. Several others were not so lucky suffering both death and injury.

If it was not the balloons, it was the enemy. On 13th November, a Ju 88 of LG1 crossed the county and whilst it did not attack any of the airfields, it was itself attacked at 2.45 pm by aircraft from No 611 (West Lancashire) Squadron. Flt Lt W. J. Leather and P/O Johnson, both flying Spitfires, engaged the Ju 88A-1 (6157) whilst it was on a reconnaissance flight of the Midlands. Attacking from both sides, the Spitfires forced the enemy to make a landing at Woodway Farm, Blewbury in Berkshire. Of the crew, Fw W. Erwin, Uffz H. Wermuth and Fw E. Zins were taken prisoner with Gefr H. Bossdorf dying after receiving bullet wounds from one of the attackers. He was later buried at Harwell, receiving a military funeral, whilst the other three crew members were taken for interrogation to Didcot Police Station. The aircraft was recovered and displayed in St Giles Street, Oxford for two weeks.

Further attacks came in March 1941, this time on the 'Q' sites thus justifying their existence, but 11th April saw Harwell once again the subject of enemy action. Two bombs were dropped initially, followed by a strafing attack before the raider turned and dropped two further bombs. Fortunately two did not explode but a third exploded by Hangar 2, luckily only causing minor damage and no loss of life. Despite this interruption, training and 'Nickelling' continued, so much so that by June 1941, No 15 OTU were the busiest and most productive in No 6 Group. The month had seen 3,040 flying hours with an output of 90 pilots, 40 observers and 80 radio operators/air gunners.

That Harwell was still a grass airfield was presenting problems, and a decision was made in July to upgrade. Approaches were made for McAlpines to construct two concrete runways, one to be 1,100 yards long and the other 1,000 yards long. From 21st July, Harwell was deemed temporarily non-operational with No 15 OTU moving to Mount Farm and the satellite at Hampstead Norris to continue their training programme. Despite the upheaval, flying did continue. For the rest of 1941, training and 'Nickelling' went on. In October, No 6 Group managed 22 'Nickel' sorties, some of them flying as far as Vichy. The new year of 1942 brought very little change to the OTU. January saw very intense training in preparation for the first of the 1,000 bomber raids. The target was to be Cologne, the first of several German cities to feel the full wrath of Bomber Command. The concept of saturation bombing came as a result of a climate of disillusion in the command when night photographs taken of previous raids had shown that not one bomb in ten fell within five miles of its intended target. With the arrival of 'Bomber' Harris at High Wycombe, the policy changed, he being a great believer in numbers for maximum devastation.

The raid was planned for the night of 30th/31st May 1942. Two days before, all personnel were confined to camp with meetings and briefings taking place under the strictest security. Harwell became a sealed unit as final preparations for the participation of the OTUs in the raid took place. It was finally decided that 20 Wellingtons of No 15 OTU would fly in the big formation.

The final hours were taken up with briefings for the aircrews whilst the groundcrews prepared the Wellingtons. As daylight faded, the last gallons of fuel were fed into the aircraft and last minute checks carried out on the bomb release mechanism. By this time the crews were in the lorries taking them to the dispersal areas where the aircraft waited. Clambering into the Wellingtons, they started the engines and awaited the signal to line up and take off. A green Very light fired from the runway control caravan arched into the air and gave the signal for off, as one by one the heavily laden Wellingtons taxied to the end of Harwell's new tarmac runway and took to the air in turn.

Crossing the North Sea, they had to endure intense cold plus attacks by German nightfighters. Most of the Continent was covered in cloud but as the bombers approached Cologne, miraculously the blanket got thinner until finally the crews were able to look down on the towns of Germany. On they went until the marker flares indicating the city of Cologne could be seen; 1,000-plus aircraft dropped their bombs and turned for home. It is impossible within these pages to give a full account of the raid but suffice to say, out of a total force of 1,046 bombers, 41 never returned.

Despite the numbers taking part, only one incident regarding aircraft being hit by bombs dropped by another aircraft above was recorded. That was an OTU Wellington but it is not known from which unit. Seventeen crews were missing from the OTU contingent, two of them

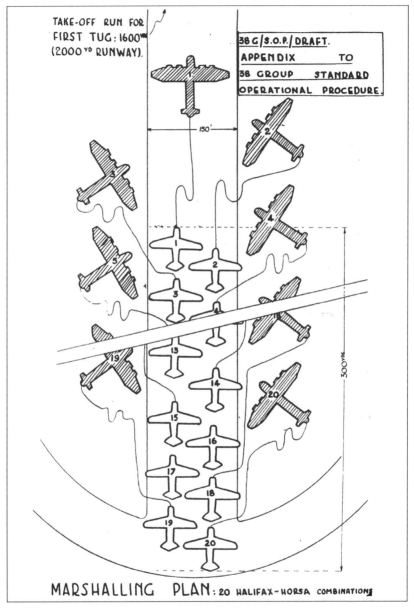

MARSHALLING PLAN: 20 HALIFAX-HORSA COMBINATIONS

Marshalling plan for take-off positions of tugs and aircraft as used at Harwell, Abingdon, Broadwell and Brize Norton. (Public Record Office)

from No 15 OTU at Harwell. When the photographic evidence of the damage was examined, it was on a far greater scale than anything yet seen. Later 1,000 bomber raids on Essen and Bremen proved to be failures due to various reasons. Once again, No 15 OTU took part and again, two Wellingtons were lost.

By August 1942, it was back to a training routine. In addition to the Wellingtons of the OTU, some overseas delivery flights of Wellingtons were being carried out from Harwell. The airfield was also being used as a departure point for bombers attacking Italian targets and among the more unusual units to use the concrete runways were two Canadian squadrons, Nos 420 (Snowy Owl) and 425 (Alouette). The delivery flights, the Italian bombing flights and the increasing Bullseye and Nickel operations of No 15 OTU were to continue for the rest of 1942 and into 1943. In October of that year the delivery and bombing flights were discontinued leaving the OTU, now flying Wellington ICs, to carry on training, adding ASR work to their programme. By December 1943, they had received Wellington Xs but their use was limited for on 3rd March 1944, No 15 OTU closed down. During its time at Harwell it had carried out the training of pilots, navigators and air gunners admirably. Now the airfield was to be given a new role, that of supporting the airborne forces as the final push to victory began.

In April 1944, Harwell became encompassed within No 38 Group, Airborne Forces. Nos 295 and 570 Squadrons flew their Armstrong Whitworth Albemarles in together with several Horsa gliders. Originally intended as a bomber, this twin-engined aircraft never operated in the role and was utilized as a glider tug and special transport for the airborne forces. No 295 Squadron was the first to receive the type at Hurn before bringing them to Harwell. It was also the first British military aircraft with a tricycle undercarriage.

'Nickelling' operations were begun on 2nd April with further sorties over the next two nights; but preparations for the planned assault on the European mainland were soon in hand when on 16th April, Exercise 'Posh' began, an exercise for dropping airborne troops and supplies. Two Albemarles of No 570 Squadron were tasked with acting as pathfinders, training by dropping troops with their supplies at Winterbourne Stoke. Further aircraft carried out the same exercise elsewhere, each one being hailed as a success upon completion. So much so that by May, the rehearsals for the greatest invasion in history were complete. The next operation would be the real thing.

One hour before midnight on 5th June 1944, three Albemarles from each squadron left Harwell. Another six were to act as pathfinders for the 6th Airborne Division, dropping men of the 22nd Independent Parachute Company at 20 minutes past midnight on 6th June. These pathfinders were to set up beacons to guide the aircraft in dropping the two parachute brigades at 50 minutes past midnight. A further twelve carried part of the main paratroop force whilst 28 Albemarles towed Horsa gliders. As the troops were released and landed in France, the aircraft returned to Harwell to commence Operation 'Mallard', the towing of loaded Horsas to Normandy.

From the beginning it had been intended that the Albemarles were just a stop-gap aircraft for the squadrons until a larger type became available. One of the first four-engined bombers to be used by Bomber Command was the Short Stirling. This was rapidly superseded by the more powerful Lancasters and had been relegated to minor roles. One of these was as a glider tug, and 19 of them arrived at Harwell on 11th July 1944. They commenced carrying out SOE drop operations until September, when the next big assault was planned. This was Operation 'Market Garden'.

As we have read at the beginning of the chapter, the newspapers described it as the 'agony of Arnhem'. The operation was intended to secure the Rhine bridgehead at Arnhem. After much argument,

The Short Stirling was often used as a glider tug. This example belongs to No 517 Squadron. (MAP)

134

General Eisenhower was at last persuaded to back Montgomery's bold plan for an armoured and airborne thrust across Holland to outflank the German defences. The operation, however, was not given all possible support. Lack of transport aircraft meant that the British paratroops were dropped piecemeal, in the midst of far stronger German forces than had been anticipated. Such troops as did reach the Rhine Bridge were wiped out and their sacrifice marked the end of any hopes of ending the war during 1944.

As far as Harwell was concerned, the drop was carried out successfully and by mid-afternoon all the Stirlings had returned safely. Immediately the groundcrews began to prepare them for the next sortie. This consisted of 13 Stirlings towing Horsas with the rest of the squadron carrying supplies which were dropped to the troops below. By the third day, the sorties were purely container drops, these lasting until 23rd September. Only then did it become evident to the crews just what a failure Arnhem had been. Further newspaper reports told the sad story.

'230 hours of hell. Struggling through a hurricane barrage of fire from 88 mm guns, tank cannon and machine-guns, the last survivors of the noble band of British Airborne troops who held the Arnhem bridgehead for nine days were ferried over to our lines during Monday night. The tragic but heroic cavalcade of bloody, mudstained, exhausted, hungry and bearded men came flooding up from the river bank into our lines after going through 230 hours of hell.

Many were stretcher cases. Many were wrapped in blankets. Some hobbled with sticks and all were so completely exhausted that they could hardly keep their eyes open. They were beaten in body but not in spirit. 'Let us get back again; give us a few tanks and we will finish the job,' they said. One of them told of the escape from the Harwell gliders. 'Most of the division dropped on Sunday. It was easy. A bit of flak hit our glider but we landed west of Oesterbeek and took up positions. The pilot had done a splendid job in getting us down in one piece as we landed amongst hedges and small trees. As the glider broke up, we piled out making sure that everyone got out safely. That was the beginning of the fireworks. The next day the situation began to deteriorate and we were forced to take up new positions.'

A General Aircraft Hamilcar after a heavy landing at Arnhem on 17th September 1944. (Public Record Office)

During one of the last drops, the fighter escort failed to materialise and sadly, four Stirlings of No 570 Squadron did not return. A further two had to force-land, but despite these incidents, for Harwell the operation to drop and supply the troops had gone according to plan and was deemed a success. By the end of the month, both squadrons had left for Rivenhall.

Harwell once again became home to an OTU when No 13 arrived

136

from Bicester on 12th October 1944 flying Bostons, Mitchells and Mosquitos. Now part of the ADGB, it also became the centre for No 2 Group TAF crews. This unit specialised in Mosquitos at Harwell but this situation changed on 1st May 1945 when No 13 OTU absorbed No 60 OTU. It was the Mitchells and Bostons of the OTU that arrived with the Mosquitos going to the satellite airfields. By the end of April 1945, the strength was 65 Mosquitos, 7 Spitfires and 15 Ansons. Flying days at Harwell however were now numbered as the end of the war approached.

The last training course was completed on 28th May 1945 as the OTU began to be run down and moved out to Middleton St George in July. The Harwell satellites were placed under Care and Maintenance and the parent airfield became the home of the School of Flight Efficiency, Transport Command followed by the Transport Command Development Unit on 1st September 1945. Both units had barely time to move in before it was decided that Harwell would cease to be an RAF airfield and would be taken over by the Ministry of Supply to became an atomic research centre.

Today this centre has become world famous in atomic research. It is a very sensitive place and it is therefore advisable to view it from a distance. Both the atomic and hydrogen bombs that Britain exploded during the 1950s owed much to the research done at Harwell. From the training of aircrews during the war to the vast atomic industry today, Harwell is continuing to earn its place in the history books.

11
KIDLINGTON

In 1919, Alan Cobham was just beginning his renowned aviation career. Flying with a company known as the Berkshire Aviation Company, one of the places he visited was Oxford. On 25th May 1933, he again came to the city this time with his National Aviation Day Tours. Two years later a return visit on 18th June once again brought flying to the attention of the public. Though it is not known precisely where in Oxford the tour landed and displayed, a fair assumption would be that it was at Kidlington. Alan Cobham was already suggesting that every major town or city in the UK should have its own municipal airport. In the case of Oxford, it is lucky enough to have Kidlington close by.

On Sunday, 3rd September 1939, with the broadcast by the then Prime Minister, Neville Chamberlain, to the effect that we were at war with Germany, all civil flying ceased in the country. Two days later, Kidlington was requisitioned by the Air Ministry. But it had already become used to a military presence as on 24th June 1938, No 26 E&RFTS had formed there flying the Hawker Audax and Hind. With the outbreak of war however, the E&RFTS were either recategorised as EFTS or were disbanded. In the case of No 26, it was the latter.

The town headquarters were retained and became the Air Ministry Code and Cypher School under the command of Wg Cdr L. T. Chandler. Use of the airfield still continued with the parent company of the Oxford Flying Club, Air Training (Oxford) Ltd, establishing a civilian repair organisation in the old flying club buildings and the Bellman hangar, recently vacated by the RAFVR, together with the hangar originally intended for the Civil Air Guard aircraft. Air Training remained at this site for just under a year before moving to new premises around the airfield perimeter. Access to the landing ground

The construction of Kidlington begins in 1939. Further hangarage soon became essential. (RAF Museum)

was still possible via a track which was cut to link both sites. With the outbreak of war, Kidlington was named as a satellite to Abingdon. On 9th September 1939, a detachment of Fairey Battles of No 52 Squadron flew in from Abingdon but stayed only for a brief period before the entire squadron moved from Upwood to Abingdon. The Bristol Blenheims of No 2 Group Pool were occasionally seen around the circuit but the first few months of war saw very little use of Kidlington.

In December 1939, control of the airfield passed to No 6 SFTS based at Little Rissington and in the bitter cold of the new year, 'E' and 'G' flights of its Advanced Training Squadron moved into Kidlington with Ansons and North American Harvards. Night flying was introduced into the training and with minimal airfield aids, accidents were bound to happen. With only a Chance light for the aircrew to identify the airfield, dark nights with no moon were to prove hazardous.

The night of 9th February 1940 was a particularly bleak one with night flying taking place in the Ansons. One aircraft, serialised N5099, crashed shortly after midnight when its pilot, a student doing several solo flights, became disorientated and struck some trees near Ensfield, sadly dying in the process. Five nights later another life was lost when a pupil was killed in a Harvard. These are but two incidents among many others, most of them involving loss of life.

The first few months of 1940 were hampered by heavy snowfalls and intense frost. Flying became very restricted as personnel were put to snow clearing duties. Drainage at the airfield was certainly not good as the snows melted and waterlogging became a problem. With the better weather however, life began to return to normal and Kidlington became an RLG controlled by No 6 SFTS. As the Battle of Britain was about to begin along the south coast, a lone enemy aircraft flew lazily across Kidlington, obviously carrying out a reconnaissance operation. Whether or not he photographed the first Hurricanes to arrive is not

The vast expansion of Kidlington is seen here around 1940. The many aircraft appear to be mainly Bristol Blenheims and Airspeed Oxfords. Very good camouflage on the hangars is also apparent. (Crown, via Air Britain)

140

known but in May, several had been received for repair by Air Training. This was to continue for six months, the rate reaching 15 a month being returned to service.

It soon became obvious to the Air Ministry that Kidlington, for its size, was certainly under used. Though of RLG or satellite status, it was destined for upgrading as the construction gangs moved in to work from March until the summer months. On 12th August 1940, Headquarters Flying Training Command decided that sufficient work had been completed to allow No 15 SFTS to be based there. Accordingly, No 6 SFTS were forced to vacate Kidlington as the first elements of No 15 arrived from Brize Norton. Gp Cpt P. E. Maitland, the CO of the school, also assumed command of Kidlington. Four more Bellman hangars were built to accommodate the 56 Harvards and two Oxfords and a large hutted camp for accommodation had been completed.

During the last days of August the rest of the unit arrived with a further 28 Harvards and two Ansons. They were followed by the headquarters staff of No 15 SFTS and by November, the entire unit was in situ. Weston-on-the-Green was acquired as a second RLG and on 13th October, the Advanced Training Squadron arrived bringing another 50 Harvards and three more Oxfords. Chipping Norton was added to the list of RLGs for with so many aircraft in one unit, Kidlington could not have operated safely.

This was a time of rapid policy changes within Flying Training Command and none more so than the order that No 15 SFTS was to change from training single-engine pilots to training multi-engine pilots. Consequently more Oxfords were received at Kidlington whilst the Harvards were sent overseas to assist the Empire Training Scheme.

With the Battle of Britain petering out in the south of the country, the enemy now turned his attention to more inland areas as Kidlington was to find out. On the afternoon of Sunday, 3rd November 1940, many people around Kidlington were out walking and taking advantage of a crisp autumn day. At around 3.15 pm, the hum of aero engines was heard approaching the airfield causing most people to look up. What they saw was the Balkan Cross and the Swastika of a Ju 88 as it came in low over the area. Opening its bomb doors, it commenced to drop five bombs. One unfortunately hit No 4 hangar, and bounced into the adjoining armoury where it exploded taking the building and its entire contents of explosives with it. It also badly damaged No 4 hangar and the one used by Air Training. In the blast,

141

one airman was killed and two others badly wounded. Two Harvards were destroyed by this one bomb whilst the other three fell on the airfield landing area. The Ju 88, still firing its guns, meanwhile had climbed into cloud cover and was lost to sight in seconds. It was a bad attack and one that shook the local people on that quiet Sunday afternoon.

In December the rain caused the field to become waterlogged as bad weather continued well into the new year. Many of the courses were delayed because of such problems, at a time when with the change-over of aircraft to Oxfords plus the greater demand for multi-engine pilots now that the Battle of Britain was over, this all greatly increased the quota of much needed bomber pilots.

January 1941 was also to become a talking point for many years to come. It was in 1930 that Amy Johnson became the darling of aviation when she flew a De Havilland Gypsy Moth from Croydon to Australia. In 1939 she joined the Air Transport Auxiliary, a gallant band of women who delivered different types of aircraft from the factories to the squadrons or from the repair units back to the squadrons. One such flight took place on Sunday, 5th January when Amy was called to pilot an Oxford from Squires Gate, Blackpool to Kidlington for No 15 SFTS.

It was a typical January day with low cloud, occasional snow showers and bitterly cold. Leaving Squires Gate at 11.50 am and climbing up through the cloud, she would have estimated to reach Kidlington at about 1.10 pm. She did not arrive, yet her proposed flight plan would have been a direct route overland with no deviations. This is the mystery that remains today, just what did happen to Amy Johnson?

Many theories have been put forward but as with Glenn Miller's disappearance, no firm conclusion has ever been reached. One which may have some substance is the fact that due to the cloud cover over all the country, Amy did not fly on a direct course but deviated and flew to the coast at Southend. Her intentions may have then been to come up the Thames Estuary and follow the Thames inland to Oxford, thus finding Kidlington just north of the city. An aircraft identified as an Oxford was seen by a convoy in the estuary to crash just off Whitstable and this may well have been the aircraft flown by Amy. Whatever happened, her body has never been found and the incident remains one of the mysteries associated with Kidlington.

The Luftwaffe paid a return visit on 27th February 1941 when a lone

Ju 88 appeared from the north. With the airfield defences blazing away, the aircraft returned the fire but did little damage before heading for cloud cover. Amidst shouts of joy, the gunners congratulated themselves on saving the day for Kidlington!

April brought an increase in the number of pilots passing out from Kidlington. May 1941 saw 6,941 flying hours achieved, a milestone that was mentioned when the Marshal of the RAF, Lord Trenchard, paid a visit to Kidlington on 30th May. At this time the building work was still continuing with seven Bellman hangars in use and plans for another one to be built. With the increase in flying, a second RLG was opened at Barford St John.

The flying training continued, though with the heavier Oxford aircraft the grass surface was suffering considerable wear and appeared to be always muddy. Headquarters Flying Training Command demanded that this condition must not persist and with the Air Ministry relenting and deciding that certain training airfields, including Kidlington, should have substantial runways, No 3 Works Squadron from Northwood moved in and commenced work. It was, in the end, only one runway that was strengthened, this being the east/west runway, 10/28. This was laid with Army Track over the grass surface which consisted of wire mesh held in place by metal discs and 24 inch steel pickets. The full complement of reinforced runways was to come some time later.

The summer period allowed day and night flying training to continue apace. That the Luftwaffe were still active over Oxfordshire can be gauged by an incident that happened on the night of 12th/13th August 1941.

The usual night-flying was taking place with the Oxfords in and out of the circuit till well after midnight. One of them was flown by a Norwegian trainee pilot, flying one of his last exercises before he was awarded his wings. He was some way from the final approach at Kidlington when he was fired upon. Noticing tracer trails flashing past, the pilot took evading action and flashed his landing lamp as the airfield came closer to indicate his intention to land. Further hits were registered on the Oxford as the wheels came down and the aircraft crossed the threshold at the airfield. Suddenly bombs were exploding on the landing area ahead but the skill of the pilot ensured that the Oxford landed safely without further damage. Shaken, he descended from the cockpit whilst the enemy made his getaway into cloud. It was later found that the Ju 88 was the same one that had also shot down an

Oxford when it infiltrated the Weston-on-the-Green circuit with the resulting death of LAC C. P. Blair.

Something of a change in aircraft type came on 30th September 1941 when No 239 Squadron flew their Curtiss Tomahawks into Kidlington from Netheravon. They remained for four days, the airfield having been allocated as an Advanced Landing Ground for the last days of Exercise 'Bumper'. The squadron flew tactical reconnaissance missions before moving on to Gatwick.

December saw Kidlington lose its RLG at Weston-on-the-Green which had been earmarked as a glider training base. This was followed by a letter from HQ Flying Training Command notifying the closure of No 15 SFTS. In its place came the formation of No 101 (Glider) Operational Training Unit. Despite much opposition from the chiefs of FTC, No 15 SFTS closed down and the instructors, aircraft and pupils moved up north to Leconfield. A week later, No 101 (G) OTU began to form at Kidlington to be ready to commence training on 1st January 1942.

Controlled by No 70 Group, Army Co-Operation Command, the

No 101 (Glider) OTU airborne over Oxfordshire towed by Hawker Hectors. (RAF Museum)

satellite at Barford St John was also taken over by this group. It was in fact this satellite that received the first four Hotspur gliders for assembly whilst Kidlington prepared itself to accommodate the first course. A short time later, it was decided that Barford St John was not suitable for glider operations and the Hotspurs were sent to Kidlington.

Sqn Ldr P. R. May was appointed to command the OTU as five Hawker Hector tug aircraft arrived. It was found that four take-offs and landings could be accomplished each hour with this number increasing after mid December when a new OTU, No 102, formed at Kidlington and commenced training. By the end of April 1942, No 101 comprised eleven Hectors, one Hind, two Audaxes and 27 Hotspurs whilst No 102 had ten Hectors, one Hind, three Audaxes and 31 Hotspurs. With such a busy airfield, accidents were bound to happen and an indication of how serious they could be is given when a Hotspur overshot a night landing and hit a parked Hurricane, sadly killing the glider instructor and injuring his pupil. Happily many other similar incidents did not result in death or injury.

By May, the army trainee pilots had arrived and the few remaining RAF had left. Their training was basically the same as the RAF. The Hector tug aircraft would taxi to the end of the runway and turn to face into the wind. Groundcrews would then attach the towing cable to the Hector and the Hotspur glider. Under the guidance of an airman, the aircraft would take up the slack until the cable was taut. With the throttle fully open, the tug would pull the glider into the air until the glider pilot released the tow cable. The Hector would then return to Kidlington, dropping the cable as it flew over the field.

A nearby grass airfield known as Glympton became an RLG together with an Emergency Landing Ground at Slade Farm. The latter, known as No 1 Satellite Landing Ground was also used in conjunction with an ELG at Starveall Farm, known as No 2 Satellite Landing Ground. The construction of a new 'Q' decoy airfield at Fawler had been completed and was used in place of the original 'Q' site at Enstone thus emphasising the importance of Kidlington as a training base.

The days for Nos 101 and 102 OTUs were however numbered and with the opening of a heavy glider conversion unit at Shrewton, they left as No 5 GTS, shortly followed by No 4 GTS formed at Kidlington. These units remained until No 5 moved to Shobdan and No 4 amalgamated with Nos 1 and 2 GTS to form No 20 (P)AFU on 10th March 1943. The days were also numbered for the elderly biplane tug aircraft that were used at Kidlington and other GTSs. Their

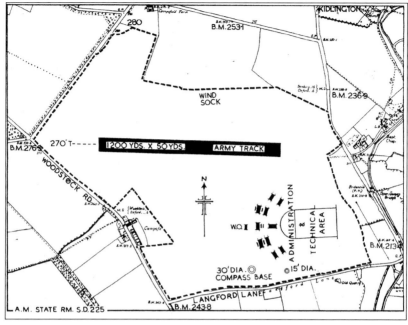

Wartime map (then secret) of Kidlington as at 1st December 1944. (Public Record Office)

replacement came in the form of the Miles Master but the biplanes were destined to soldier on for some further months.

Yet again a wet winter proved a problem for the airfield with waterlogging. With just one runway completed in army track, and with a busy schedule of courses to complete, further efforts to persuade the Air Ministry to lay tracking on the other runways fell upon deaf ears. In order to ease the congestion at Kidlington and therefore the constant use of the runways, Kingston Bagpuize was sanctioned as an additional satellite. Its use in this respect was very minimal as an order was received stating that all glider training was to cease at Kidlington. On 2nd March 1943, any uncompleted courses were transferred to Weston-on-the-Green and the airfield repair work was duly put in hand.

Before the work began, No 411 (Grizzly Bear) Canadian Squadron flew their Spitfires in from Digby for two days of exercises. They were joined by No 167 (Gold Coast) Squadron who flew their Spitfire VCs in from Ludham. Commanded by Sqn Ldr N. N. Bretz and Sqn Ldr A. C. Stewart respectively, the two squadrons flew patrols throughout Oxfordshire before moving to Fowlmere.

Whilst they were at Kidlington, part of the exercise involved the airfield being 'attacked' by Spitfires of No 616 (South Yorkshire) Squadron who reported a concentration of around 30 Spitfires and 15 Mustangs, the latter belonging to the Air Training repair unit. Sadly the exercise was not without its tragedy when two Spitfires of No 616 collided north-west of Oxford, one of them crashing at Kidlington. Both pilots were killed. With the departure of the Spitfires, Kidlington was once again left to the training courses of No 20 (P)AFU.

The training continued during 1944 with an average output of 150 pupils per month. As the build up to victory began, so the demand and output of pilots began to slowly decrease. In December 1944, Gp Cpt D. P. Hanafin DFC, AFC took command of both Kidlington and No 20 (P)AFU from Gp Cpt Noakes. By 1st March 1945, training was no longer required and the airfield and the villages around prepared to celebrate the forthcoming VE day.

Modern Kidlington, now known as Oxford Airport, supports many flying clubs. It is operated by CSE (Aviation) Ltd.

147

By 31st May 1945, Kidlington, Weston-on-the-Green and No 20 (P)AFU were closed down and in June a non-flying unit, No 1 Aircrew Holding Unit took over the airfield. Peacetime military units to use the site included No 60 Group GL Calibration Unit, later renamed the Air Position Plotting Unit, and No 53 Signals Unit together with the reformed Oxford University Air Squadron. The civilian Oxford Aeroplane Club formed at Kidlington when the University Air Squadron moved out. The present operators of the airfield, CSE (Aviation) Ltd, have made great improvements and it is now a major player for light and executive aviation within the region. Now known as Oxford (Kidlington) Airport, it still continues in the training role that was pursued during the war years, being the first CAA school approved for Commercial Pilot License training. From glider to power flight training, Kidlington is set to continue into the foreseeable future.

12
MOUNT FARM

It was not in fact the existence or the exploits of a wartime airfield that placed Mount Farm on the map but a discovery made originally many years earlier. It was a Major Allen during the 1930s who, during a flight over the area, took photographs which when developed, showed signs of an ancient settlement on the northern side of the later airfield. Apart from mapping it for his own interest, nothing further was done until after the Second World War when the land had been returned to its original owners. It was during 1978 that a resurgence of interest came about and the Oxford Archaeological Unit began to explore the area. Since that time they have found numerous artefacts from the Bronze and Iron Ages including a skeleton in a primitive burial site. Time was at a premium as a national company were planning to excavate gravel from the old airfield but the unit was given sufficient time to find numerous other relics, including cartridge cases and shells from the war.

It was the increased use by No 12 OTU of nearby Benson that had caused a satellite airfield to be built eight miles south-east of Oxford and five miles north-west of Benson. Initially referred to as Dorchester, it was later named RAF Mount Farm and was ready for use by July 1940. From the beginning it was intended to have a concrete main runway running north-east to south-west together with two secondary ones. Though the laying of the runways was not completed until November 1940, it was a grade up on its parent station of Benson which at that time was still totally grass. There were however no permanent buildings for the personnel posted to the base. By mid-August, Mount Farm was already undergoing a major expansion including the hard runways and brick-built accommodation.

From the beginning, the Fairey Battles of No 12 OTU from Benson had been using the new satellite. By this time the type was reaching the end of its life and with the Vickers Wellington becoming the mainstay of Bomber Command, No 12 OTU were due for these to replace the Battles. Benson as we have seen was still grass and when it rained, this became waterlogged. This was no good for training purposes but with the completion of the runways at Mount Farm, this enabled the OTU to operate Wellingtons and Ansons from December 1940, including being used for day and night flying. It also changed from a medium bomber OTU to a half-heavy bomber OTU.

The Christmas period over, it was back to the rigorous task of training bomber crews. With the new aircraft it was not only the trainee crews and their instructors that had to get used to a twin-engined bomber but the groundcrews as well. Several mishaps sadly occurred, with one at Mount Farm involving an airman groundcrew. Forgetting that unlike the Battles, the Wellington had two propellers, he walked directly into one that was revolving. Several further mishaps were to

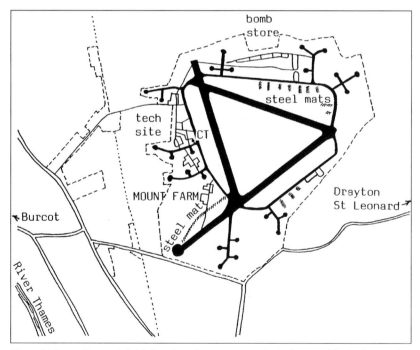

Plan of Mount Farm airfield showing the runway and site layout. (Chris Samson)

happen at the parent station together with several crashes as the Benson chapter recalls.

The Wellington had been widely welcomed after the Battle of Britain for with its geodetic construction, it was able to take some harsh punishment in the hands of novice crews. Pilots arriving at operational squadrons direct from an OTU usually had about 30 hours under their belt and were then required to do five trips on operations as second pilot with an experienced crew to learn the ropes. Many did not make it and were forced to remuster for other aircrew duties such as gunner etc. The only interruption to flying training at Mount Farm came whenever an enemy aircraft was known to be in their area, as an incident in February 1941 shows.

The morning training on Thursday, 27th February had gone well, despite the low cloud that hung over the UK most of the day allowing only moderate visibility. With much of the Continent under similar conditions, German activity was very low. The daylight operations by the enemy were restricted to minor weather and shipping reconnaissance flights with a few inland penetrations by single aircraft taking advantage of the cloud cover. One such aircraft travelled inland and bombed Grantham, killing 15 people. It was possibly the same aircraft that dropped two bombs about half a mile from Mount Farm. Flying in the vicinity of the airfield it gave the light ack-ack guns on airfield defence duties an opportunity to show their prowess. With guns blazing they forced the raider to turn away and head towards Benson. At least they had the satisfaction of frightening him off!

A second attack during night-flying saw 13 50-kg bombs dropped, this being far more devastating than the afternoon incident. One badly cratered the north-east/south-west runway with two others making a mess of the perimeter track. Sadly one NCO was killed with a further three airmen seriously injured. Damage was also done to two Wellingtons and a Magister. The next morning was given over to assessing the damage and repairing the cratered runway. The damaged aircraft were removed and by the next day, flying could be resumed. It had given the Mount Farm personnel their first taste of war but it was not to be the last. The week after the attack was a melancholy period at the base as the airman who was killed in the raid was buried with full military honours.

The next two months were fairly peaceful but Sunday, 12th May saw another large raid materialise. The morning dawned fair with minor attacks on shipping during the day, but by night a different story emerged. It was Luftflotte 3 that were concerned with attacks on airfields in an armada that employed over 240 aircraft. The cities of Exeter and Portsmouth together with 20 airfields were intended targets. In Oxfordshire, Harwell and Bicester were on that list but were not found. Instead, it was Mount Farm that was hit when a bomb once again dropped on the main runway causing a 50 foot crater to appear. Others fell on the perimeter track damaging it badly whilst some bombs fell on waste ground within the airfield boundaries. Once again it was everyone to the shovels in order to get the airfield serviceable.

The 12th June 1941 saw the first 'Nickelling' sorties to be flown from Mount Farm, followed by several others. These were not without incident for one Wellington was lost, killing four crew members on one of the last sorties before orders were received that No 12 OTU were to move to RAF Chipping Warden in Northamptonshire.

From one OTU to another, as No 15 at Harwell took over the control of Mount Farm on 23rd July 1941, but with the increase in PR squadrons at Benson, it returned to the fold of its former parent station in January 1942. On 23rd January, four Spitfires of No 140 Squadron moved over to Mount Farm to be permanently based there as part of the Photographic Reconnaissance unit. During May, the rest of the squadron moved there while the laying of concrete runways went on at Benson. In addition, the Blenheims of No 140 Squadron and the station Tiger Moth moved in, the former to carry out sorties by night. It was now a very busy time at Mount Farm for with the run-up to Operation 'Jubilee' – the Dieppe landings – the Spitfires were photographing the entire area by day with the Blenheims flying night reconnaissance sorties. On one day alone, the Spitfires flew 22 sorties, most of them over Dieppe.

The rest of 1942 and early 1943 saw the main squadron return to Benson with Mount Farm being used once again as more of a satellite airfield. This status did not prevent it from being used as an emergency landing ground, for any day or night of the year would see a large variety of bombers sitting around the perimeter all showing signs of battle damage. The days, however, of RAF occupation were drawing to a close as 15th March 1943 saw No 140 Squadron move to Hartford Bridge Blackbushe (see *Hampshire Airfields in the Second World War*). It was not the use of the airfield that was to change in the coming year but the occupants, for Mount Farm was to become Station 234 of the United States 8th Army Air Force.

The 13th Photographic Reconnaissance Squadron had been activated on 20th June 1942 in Colorado Springs (it was redesignated the 13th Photographic Squadron (Light) on 6th February 1943, only to revert to its former title on 13th November 1943). The main group sailed for the UK in November and arrived at Podington on 2nd December 1942 to be followed by its aircraft, mainly P-38 and F-5 Lightnings, the next week. On 16th February 1943, the 13th PR Squadron moved to Mount Farm and became a unit within the 7th Photographic Reconnaissance and Mapping Group.

From a relatively quiet base, Mount Farm now became a very noisy one much to the dismay of local people. Powered by two 1,475 hp Allison engines, the Lightning was the ultimate American long-range fighter and fighter/bomber of the period. Out of a total production of 9,923 aircraft, around 1,000 were stripped of their nose guns and instead carried a battery of five cameras. The group were mainly concerned with photographing possible landing sites along the Normandy coast in preparation for an Allied landing during 1944. The unit's purpose had been caricatured in the emblem or crest, which was a diving black cat with yellow eyes and a light red tongue, holding a black aerial camera. Only the Americans could have such crests! In addition to the Lightnings, the unit also had several L-4 Piper Cubs on strength for ferry and light duties.

A rather surprising move came in late 1943 when the 13th PR received Spitfires, in a reverse lend-lease move. These were mainly used for obtaining photographs of damage inflicted by the 8th AAF bomb groups. Additional work involved providing a mapping service for air and ground units as well as observing and reporting on enemy movements and obtaining data on weather conditions.

Emblem of the 13th Photographic Reconnaissance Squadron. (Chris Samson)

153

With this very busy airfield in the midst of a rural community, a liaison committee was set up to promote relations between the locals and the influx of American servicemen. Some had already opened their homes to the 'Yanks' and dances and gatherings to foster this relationship became commonplace.

On 12th May 1943, another American unit arrived at Mount Farm. This time it was the 14th PR Squadron who brought their P-38s and F-5s in, followed by another unit a month later, the 22nd PR Squadron. A fourth squadron, No 27, joined Mount Farm on 4th November 1943, all these units becoming part of the 7th Photographic Group (Reconnaissance) under the command of Colonel James G. Hall. The group were now very busy photographing airfields, cities, industrial establishments and ports in France, the Low Countries and Germany as the run-up to D-Day, 6th June 1944 commenced.

By 1944, the Spitfires were even roaming as far as Berlin in preparation for the victory that everyone hoped would come with the forthcoming invasion. Over D-Day itself and after, the group were photographing enemy movements, bridges, marshalling yards, canals, highways and other numerous targets, all of which contributed to the success of the Normandy landings. It was during this period that the 7th Photographic Group (Reconnaissance) earned a Distinguished Unit Citation. Now, with the invasion well forward, sorties were switched to gathering information regarding the V-1 sites.

Command of the unit had passed to Lt Col Norris E. Hartwell, who in turn handed the reins over to Lt Col Clarence A. Shoop on 9th August 1944. The award of the French Croix de Guerre with Palm during 1944 was a testament to the photographic work done over France and the success of the landings. Reconnaissance was now connected with the airborne attack on Holland during September and for the Battle of the Bulge which lasted from December 1944 to January 1945. For this campaign the group received a number of P-51 Mustangs to escort the reconnaissance aircraft as the enemy appeared to be throwing in all his fighters in a last desperate attempt to turn the tide of the war.

It was Colonel George W. Humbricht who led the 7th PG(R) in the months to final victory. The group supported the Allied drive across the Rhine and into Germany and took part in the final bomb-damage assessment. As No 27 Squadron left Mount Farm for France and later the nearby airfield of Chalgrove, Christmas 1944 was one to celebrate and this the Americans did in style at Mount Farm.

The festivities over, it was back to work for the 7th as the Lightnings, Spitfires and Mustangs went on with their photographing and mapping of the Continent. This continued up to and beyond VE Day, until the HQ of the 7th moved to Chalgrove on 8th April 1945 followed in December by the remaining three squadrons. Suddenly and quickly, the Americans had left Mount Farm. It was returned to the RAF on 1st May 1945 and resumed its status as a satellite to Benson.

No 8 OTU moved in briefly but the flying days at the base were numbered. For a year after the departure of the OTU it became a store for surplus military vehicles but was reduced to Care and Maintenance shortly after and returned to farming. What buildings there were came under the demolition men as farming continued around the destruction. In 1957 the site was sold to an aggregate company who began to extract gravel.

Little of Mount Farm remains today but beside the perimeter of the airfield is a magnificent memorial to the people who served there, formed from a Spitfire propeller set in concrete. The inscription is dedicated to the 7th Photographic Group (Reconnaissance), who were inactivated on 21st November 1945. This at least is a lasting tribute to a once very active airfield.

The memorial situated at Mount Farm.

155

13

UPPER HEYFORD

The Vickers Wellesley was the first RAF aircraft to employ geodetic construction, later to be used in the construction of the Wellington bomber. The aircraft was built as a private venture and was a development of a general purpose biplane. Designated Air Ministry Spec G.4/31, it first flew on 19th June 1935 and in September, the Air Ministry ordered 96. Between March 1937 and May 1938, 176 Wellesleys were built, the first entering service with No 76 Squadron at Finningley in April 1937.

Being a single-engined bomber, it was quickly overtaken by the twin-engined larger aircraft such as the Hampden, Whitley and the aforementioned Wellington. Its fame however, came with the breaking of the World Long Distance Record which the type achieved with the RAF Long Range Development Flight in 1938. Formed under the command of Wg Cdr O. R. Gayford, on 5th November, three modified Wellesleys, s/n's L2638, L2639 and L2680, led by Sqn Ldr R. Kellett, took off from Ismailia (Egypt) to fly to Darwin non-stop. Fitted with special Pegasus engines and with a 1,290 fuel capacity, they broke the standing record and achieved their place in the history of the RAF. The Long Range Development Flight was at that time based at Upper Heyford.

The airfield's origins dated back to the First World War. Situated five miles north-west of Bicester, it was not completed until 1918 and did not really see action before the armistice was signed. On 3rd November 1918, No 123 Squadron reformed at Heyford, the first to do so here. This was a Canadian-manned fighter squadron which was redesignated No 2 Squadron of the Canadian Air Force. At the time of reforming it was equipped with Sopwith Dolphins, the first of the

No 2 Squadron Canadian Air Force, at Upper Heyford from November 1918 to March 1919. This unit was originally No 123 Squadron RAF. (Frank Cheesman)

Sopwith Scouts to have an in-line engine in place of the more usual rotary. These were rapidly exchanged for the DH.9A which the squadron took to Shoreham in Sussex in March 1919. No 81 Squadron had also arrived at Upper Heyford at the same time. Redesignated No 1 Squadron, Canadian Air Force, they were similarly Dolphin equipped, taking these to Shoreham at the same time.

With the departure of both squadrons, Upper Heyford closed. For some years it was allowed to decay but the 1924 Defence Review, the forerunner to the vast expansion programme, saw the base reopen as a bomber station in October 1927. The Station Flight was formed with three Avro 504Ns allowing the Oxford University Air Squadron to commence flying training. No 10 Squadron was reformed on 3rd January 1928 and No 99 Squadron flying their Handley Page Hyderabads in from Bircham Newton on 5th January 1928. A heavy night bomber of the 1920s, the type first flew in October 1923. No 99 were the first squadron to be equipped with the Hyderabad. Both units soon converted to the Handley Page Hinaidi, a converted Hyderabad, No 99 being again the first squadron to receive it. No 10 Squadron meanwhile, took their Hinaidis to Boscombe Down on 1st April 1931 whilst No 99 further converted to the Handley Page Heyford and took them to Mildenhall on 15th November 1934. These were the last stages of the heavy biplane bombers as Upper Heyford was about to enter a new era.

Meanwhile, further squadrons had rotated through the base. No 40 Squadron reformed there on 1st April 1931. They were equipped with the first Fairey Gordons to enter RAF service but immediately moved over to Abingdon. No 18 (Burma) Squadron reformed at the base on 20th October 1931 equipped with the lighter Hawker Hart biplane bomber, which was to prove to be one of the most adaptable biplanes ever to enter service with the RAF. Working up on the aircraft commenced immediately enabling No 18 Squadron to take part in the 1933 RAF Hendon Display with a flying display of wing drill. Two years later they repeated the exercise and became well known for precision flying. On 7th January 1936 they moved to Bircham Newton and converted to Hawker Hinds before bringing them back to Upper Heyford on 7th September 1936. Conversion to the Bristol Blenheim I took place in March 1938 and the squadron was to remain at Heyford until the outbreak of war.

No 57 Squadron had flown their Hawker Harts into the base on 5th September 1932. They would similarly convert to the Hind and the Blenheim before leaving just after the war started. With the expansion period now at full pace, a need for more squadrons arose as many squadrons and units rotated through Upper Heyford. Nos 58 and 215 Squadrons flew Vickers Virginias before moving to newly completed Driffield. No 218 (Gold Coast) Squadron had reformed from 'C' Flight of No 57 Squadron whilst 'B' Flight of No 57 was taken as the nucleus for No 108 Squadron. When they left for Farnborough in April 1937, the new 'B' Flight of No 57 Squadron then became No 226 Squadron which moved to Harwell in April 1937. With No 113 Squadron reforming at Upper Heyford on the 18th May 1937 with Hawker Hinds and then taking them to Grantham two months later, it was certainly a period of rapid change.

It was however 1938 that really became the year for Upper Heyford when the Long Range Development Flight became residents. As we have already read, the rather ungainly looking Vickers Wellesley achieved fame by beating the world distance record of 6,306 miles set the year previous by a Russian Antonov 25. The three Wellesleys flown by Sqn Ldr Kellet, Flt Lt Hogan and Flt Lt Combe, left Egypt on 5th November 1938 and two days later, two of the aircraft, flown by Kellett and Combe, arrived in Darwin to a rapturous welcome. Sadly Flt Lt

158

Flying from Upper Heyford, the Vickers Wellesley was the aircraft used by the Long Range Development Flight. Their record breaking flight of 7,157 miles remained unbeaten until after the war. Pictured is an aircraft of No 35 Squadron.

Hogan had to land at Kupanc, Timor to refuel. The pilots were in the air for 48 hours and achieved a distance of 7,157.7 miles. Back at Upper Heyford, the news was welcomed with great elation, especially at this time of growing international tension between Germany and the rest of Europe including Great Britain. For the Wellesley, it was really its swansong for it was later relegated to shipping reconnaissance duties as the newer and larger bombers came on stream.

By 1938, it had become obvious to many that the fast pace of the military organisation in Germany could not be stopped. The immense build-up of the Luftwaffe, which by 1935 comprised a total of 1,888 aircraft of all types, continued unabated. One by one the masks of the 'flying clubs' came off and they were handed over to the newly formed Luftwaffe. In August 1936, it went into battle for the first time in support of General Franco's Nationalist Forces rebelling against the Spanish Republican Communist Government. The Luftwaffe was allowed to develop its own fighter and bomber tactics for use in any future war, the idea of which was already festering in the minds of Hitler and his generals. All of this was seen by the outside world but very little was done to stop it.

At Upper Heyford, an air of urgency about the international situation was apparent. The monoplane era arrived in the form of the Blenheim when No 57 Squadron received them in March 1938. Further Blenheims arrived when No 34 Squadron came in from Lympne and converted to the type. With No 18 (Burma) Squadron giving up their Hinds in May 1939 for a further complement of Blenheims, all three

159

squadrons were resident during the Munich Crisis of 1939 and were scheduled to become part of the AASF for France.

On 30th September 1938, the Prime Minister, Neville Chamberlain, gaunt and exhausted, returned from his final meeting with Hitler. Waving a piece of paper he proclaimed 'Peace for our time'. It was hoped that with the agreement giving Hitler the power to march into Czechoslovakia, war would be averted. On 17th March 1939, Hitler told the world that Czechoslovakia had ceased to exist. On 31st March, Chamberlain announced the Anglo/French guarantee to Poland and by August had warned Hitler that Britain would fulfill its obligations should Poland be threatened. On 1st September 1939, Poland was invaded by the Germans. War was now inevitable.

On the eve, Upper Heyford was placed under the control of No 6 Group and into a training role. A satellite airfield was set up at Brackley and both Blenheim squadrons, Nos 18 and 57, prepared to move to France in the hope of helping stop the expected German onslaught. A broadcast was relayed throughout the base telling all the personnel that we were now at war and to carry side-arms, for those authorised to do so, at all times.

The first Handley Page Hampdens to be seen at Upper Heyford arrived when Nos 7 and 76 Squadrons flew in from Finningley on 23rd September 1939. They formed No 5 Group Pool but were soon to form the nucleus of No 16 OTU. In the training role, the Hampden found a better niche than as a bomber. It was the Air Staff who had decided that the Hampden should operate as a day bomber, but this was to prove disastrous as the protective fire-power of the aircraft proved totally inadequate against German fighters. Cramped conditions for the crew also led to fatigue on long flights. Production of the Hampden ceased with the 500th coming off the line in July 1940, but it did serve with No 16 OTU for some considerable time. The unit also received the Handley Page Hereford, an up-rated version of the Hampden. This mark also served briefly as a bomber but once again, was mainly employed as a bomber-crew trainer with No 16 OTU.

Although only a training station, it was a very hectic and busy one. Accidents were not usually serious considering the amount of flying training that was taking place but one incident will act as a reminder of what could and certainly did happen on occasions. Tuesday, 13th August, known as 'Eagle Day' for the Battle of Britain being fought above the south-east counties, dawned mainly fair with early morning mist. This turned into a light drizzle around midday when two

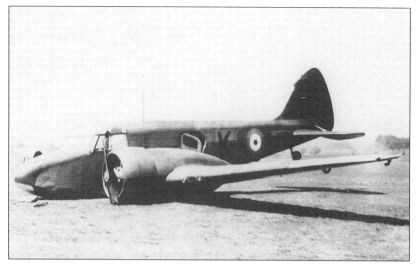

One of many casualties experienced by the OTUs. An Airspeed Oxford suffers a heavy landing.

Hampdens, L4138 and P4339, were scheduled for a training sortie. Why they were using different runways is not recorded but just as both were getting airborne, they somehow collided with the result that both aircraft fell to the ground, bursting into flames.

Like most OTUs, No 16 was also tasked with 'Nickelling' operations to give trainee crews operational experience. The first of these took place on 25th and 27th July 1940 with several more following in August. Their 'bomb load' was 13 tons of paper made into leaflets which were dropped over the occupied countries. Even at this early stage of the war, propaganda was part of the action. Printed mainly in French, Dutch, German and Italian, when released they slowly fluttered down to earth in the hope of perhaps shortening the war.

With the Battle of Britain raging to the south, Oxfordshire was very little affected. The occasional raider was seen over Oxford itself, Saturday, 5th October 1940 being one of these times. There were four attacks that day on the country, one of them being around 2.15 am when about 20 enemy aircraft were operating over the Midlands and South East. Several aircraft however broke away from the main formations, one of them coming into the county and dropping its bombs on Oxford. Very little damage was sustained as they fell mainly on waste ground. Within minutes the 'all clear' sounded and people went back to bed. Only on rare occasions during the Battle were the Oxfordshire airfields singled out for major attacks by the Luftwaffe.

The need now arose for additional satellites with nearby Croughton serving this purpose. Night flying began on an intense scale coupled with further 'Nickelling' operations throughout the rest of the year. As 1940 ended and the new year arrived, No 16 OTU still continued training Hampden crews. The Herefords had proved totally unreliable for the punishment that any aircraft would receive from a crew under training and were sent for use elsewhere. The aircraft strength for the OTU now stood at 49 Hampdens, 13 Ansons, 12 Oxfords and several light aircraft. A new satellite airfield, Barford St John, would come into use in 1942 with additional use being made of Hinton-in-the-Hedges.

With the Battle of Britain now over, the Luftwaffe turned its attention to raids on the British mainland. The night of Wednesday, 12th/13th March 1941 saw the airfield attacked by a single raider. With dusk falling at 7.15 pm, several major attacks developed over the country. Whilst one of the main attacks carried out by Luftflotte 3 was on Merseyside, a lone He 111 found Upper Heyford and dropped its bombs. Damage was done to the landing area and to some of the aircraft sitting at dispersal but there was no loss of life. Again on Friday, 9th/10th May, the night-time attacks were far ranging with 89

Handley Page Hampdens of No 16 OTU airborne from Upper Heywood. (MAP via Peter Davis)

Heinkel He 111. It was this type that was responsible for some of the attacks on Oxfordshire airfields. (MAP)

long range bombers and 19 long range fighter/bombers attacking a variety of targets including Upper Heyford. This time it was a Ju 88 of KG1 that found the airfield and commenced to drop its bombs. In seconds, the devastation was done and the aircraft climbed to safety and headed for the Channel coast. Though these lone raids caused no casualties, they were certainly a reminder of just what many other airfields had suffered and what many cities were suffering now, night after night.

Training continued throughout 1941 and into 1942. Crew output was stepped up as the bomber raids on Germany increased for it was the belief of Air Marshal Arthur Harris, who had taken over as the C-in-C Bomber Command on 22nd February 1941, that the war might be brought to a quicker end by the constant bombardment of Germany. Bomber aircraft production had increased substantially whilst the output of crews to fly them had not kept pace. Orders went out that the OTUs were to train more crews and quicker. As if to emphasise the orders of Harris, No 16 OTU received its first Wellington ICs. This was a great advance on the aging Hampdens and resulted in Upper Heyford increasing its crew output.

With the war now firmly being carried back to the enemy, 26th

Air Chief Marshal Sir Arthur 'Bomber' Harris, C-in-C Bomber Command 1942–1945. (Imperial War Museum – ref. CH13020)

March 1942 heard Winston Churchill declare, 'It now seems very likely that we and our allies cannot lose this war – except through our own fault.' He went on, 'The British nation, stirred and moved by their own experiences as never before in their history, are determined to conquer or die.' The last word was certainly in mind as plans were formulated for the first 1,000 bomber raid on a German city.

It was at the Commander-in-Chief's residence, a large Victorian house known as 'Springfield' just outside Uxbridge, that the idea for such a raid was born. One pleasant evening in May 1941, Harris was entertaining several high ranking officers including his Senior Air Staff Officer, Air Vice-Marshal R.H.M.S Saundby. Harris was complaining about the lack of concentrated bombing and asked Saundby how long it was going to be before a really crushing force could be mustered, somewhere around 1,000. Saundby answered, 'We could do it now, you know.'

'Nonsense,' replied Harris.

'But we could, you know, if we make use of the conversion and training planes using instructors and if necessary, pupil crews. I think we could do it.' The seed had been sown.

In May 1942, No 16 OTU was half equipped with Wellingtons and was detailed to take part in the first of the 1,000 bomber raids. Behind locked doors, the crews were briefed. They had been left to sort themselves out regarding crew members, for a natural self-selection process was better than being forced to join a particular crew only to find that you did not fit in. A similar situation was taking place at 19 other OTUs at the same time as at Upper Heyford. No 16 OTU were able to put up 14 Wellingtons and 16 Hampdens for the raid on Cologne which took place over the night of 31st May. In the end, just 868 aircraft managed to bomb Cologne, dropping 1,455 tons of explosives. More than 5,000 people were killed or injured with 45,000 left homeless. The era of saturation bombing had begun.

Back at Upper Heyford, the crews that took part in the raid were carefully debriefed. For them it had been first time experience and one they would have to get used to. For the 1,000 bomber raid on Essen over the night of 1st and 2nd of June, 30 crews were from No 16 OTU. Bremen was next on the list at the end of June in which 23 Wellington crews took part. With further bombing raids taking place during July, August and September 1942, experience was being gained all the time for the trainee crews. Not so for the groundcrews who throughout this period continued to work to a pattern, as Douglas Neil recalled.

'Having spent time at RAF Warboys and a few months at RAF Wing, I was posted to Upper Heyford in June 1942 and became part of 'B' Flight as Flight Mechanic Engines on Wellingtons. The course for the trainee aircrews lasted two weeks with our flight and consisted of cross country navigation, bombing, camera bombing and air firing at a target drogue. Us groundcrew had to work in shifts, day shift, night flying shift and early and late shift. It wasn't so bad in the summer months but winter was the worst time when it seemed to be either raining or freezing or both. Then the worst job of all was spreading de-icing paste over the leading edge of the mainplanes when your hands were frozen and keeping your fingers away from the balloon cable cutter. Almost as bad was trying to stop from sliding down the icy mainplanes while refuelling.

I did a couple of months at Barford St John, the satellite airfield, where the main interest was the prototype of a jet single-seater fighter which was kept in one of the hangars. When the test pilot came in flying a Hurricane, all normal flying was suspended. The same applied when the jet was airborne and we were told not to leave our dispersal until it had landed and had been padlocked in the hangar.

One of the bad memories that I have was when a staff pilot took

'B' Flight of No 16 OTU in front of one of the Wellingtons in 1943. Doug Neil is standing in the back row, seventh from the left. (Doug Neil)

a 'Wimpey' up for an air test and took a Corporal groundcrew as a passenger. At the end of the test as he flew low level over the runway, one of the mainplanes broke off at the engine nacelle and the aircraft crashed just off the end of the runway. The pilot managed to bail out, his parachute opening just before he hit the ground and I think his only injury was a broken ankle. Sadly his passenger didn't make it and was killed in the crash. I think it was about this time that cracks were found in the main spar of some Wellingtons and this led to modifications being carried out. It all seems a long time ago now although at times just like yesterday.'

The constant use at Upper Heyford made it clear it could not cope without hard runways. The HQ moved to Barford St John from March to December 1942 whilst John Laing & Son Ltd constructed the runways to class A standard; one main runway 2,000 yards long and two subsidiaries 1,400 yards long.

Most of the Hampdens had gone by early 1943 and in March, the OTU's strength stood at 57 Wellington ICs, six Ansons, a Defiant and two Lysanders. These were now joined by No 1473 Flight, a very 'hush-hush' radio countermeasures unit. Flying Wellingtons and Ansons and commanded by Flt Lt C. F. Grant DFC, it monitored German radio and radar transmissions which the enemy were using, amongst other things, to assist their aircraft in accurate bombing. No 16 OTU were now receiving Wellington IIIs and with them came an order that four 'Nickelling' sorties were to be flown every fortnight. This pattern continued throughout the autumn of 1943 with the OTU exchanging their Mk IIIs for the Wellington X in November. This mark was the last of the bomber variants with 3,804 being delivered for service. The Mark X was to serve with the RAF until 1953, a proud record for a fine aeroplane.

By 8th February 1944, the plan for 'Overlord' had been confirmed at Allied HQ and six days later, General Eisenhower had established the HQ of SHAEF. The countdown to the conquering of the enemy had begun. This news however and the eventual assault on the Normandy coast had little effect on Upper Heyford where the training of crews continued. Although only at the airfield for a brief period, the experiences of Ricky Dyson were typical of many of the trainees.

'I was stationed at Upper Heyford from early April until early June 1944. In those days it was No 16 OTU and its satellite airfield

167

was Barford St John from where I did most of my flying. I arrived fresh from gunnery school proudly wearing my AG brevet and eager to fly in the rear turret of the Wellington bomber. Upper Heyford was brick-built with a very comfortable sergeants' mess, unlike the hutted buildings at Barford St John. The bombing range we used was Preston Capes and the 'watering holes' were Bloxham and Banbury and of course, Oxford.

On the second day of my arrival I got 'crewed up' and met a tall young Aussie pilot, Desmond Kelly, more commonly known as 'Ned'. We had all assembled in an empty hangar and the pilots were asked to select a crew of their choice. When Ned approached me, he had already selected most of his crew and we all met in the sergeants' mess later when I accepted to be his rear gunner. Of course, as far as I was concerned, he had chosen the best crew in the whole of Bomber Command. The course consisted of

One of the OTU crews at Upper Heyford. Ricky Dyson is in the back row far right. (R. Dyson)

navigational exercises, practice bombing, cross country gunnery exercises and much more. We also went out dropping leaflets over France etc and on occasions, took part in the 1,000 bomber raids. I was one of the lucky ones who came back, sadly many did not.'

A new unit, No 1655 Mosquito Training Unit had arrived by the end of the year equipped with Mosquitos and Oxfords. This new unit was absorbed into No 16 OTU. Coming under the control of No 92 Group, 45 Mosquitos were used for the training of crews for medium and high level bomber squadrons. From this time until and after Victory in August 1945, the task of the OTU continued, until it moved to Cottesmore in March 1946.

It was now a different kind of war, known as the 'Cold War', and the countries of the Eastern Bloc were the supposed enemy. With this supposition, 1st June 1951 saw control of Upper Heyford pass to the USAF and the 7509th Air Base Squadron. The first permanent squadon was the 328th Bomb Squadron with 15 B-50Ds. The 93rd Air Refuelling Group arrived for a 90 day stay in December of the same year. In 1955 the first nuclear-capable B-47B Stratojets in the UK arrived, the largest aircraft to be seen at the base up to that time. In 1966 they were replaced by the 66th Tactical Reconnaisance Wing with RF-101C Voodoos. Later would come the controversial F-IIIEs of the 20th Tactical Fighter Wing which remained until the ending of the 'Cold War' during the early 1990s. With this came a large reduction in the American forces stationed in the UK and the eventual closure of Upper Heyford.

In 1985 a memorial stone was erected in the village of Upper Heyford to commemorate all those killed flying from the base. A further memorial was placed alongside the original in 1997, dedicated to all those who lost their lives flying with No 16 OTU. In 1994 the airfield was placed in the Defence Land Agent's hands for disposal, eventually going the way that so many wartime airfields have sadly done. There are plans to redevelop the site as an urban village.

From its roots in the first conflict to its training role in the second and its peacetime association with the USAF, Upper Heyford has earned its place in the history of Oxfordshire.

14
WATCHFIELD

In today's modern aviation, the ILS or Instrument Landing System is taken for granted at most international airports and military bases. It enables aircraft to land safely in practically any weather conditions at any particular time of the year. This was not the case pre-war. One of the airfields used in the research and development and the eventual introduction of 'blind flying', as it was then called, was Watchfield which is situated six miles north of Swindon.

The basic life-saver at the beginning and which continued through-out the war was a system known as 'Darky'. This was a method by which an aircraft could ask for a homing bearing using the call sign 'Darky'. A transmitter/receiver was in operation on most RAF stations and by taking bearings, they were able to fix the position of any aircraft and pass the appropriate information on to the troubled pilot. Another method to help lost pilots was to arrange searchlight beams, usually three, to be directed upwards to form a cone. These became known as 'Sandra Lights' and when reflected on a low cloud base, were certainly an asset to lost pilots.

The only airfield approach aid in use during the early part of the war was the civilian 'ZZ' system. This depended on the pilot setting the local barometric pressure correctly on his altimeter and taking and using the 'direction finding' aid to overfly the airfield. After a set time, the pilot then reversed his course and with continuing assistance from the 'direction finding' aid at the airfield, would then descend and land. All of this, however, was very hit and miss until the 'Blind Approach School' was established at Watchfield on 17th October 1940.

With the building of Watchfield completed by July 1940, No 3 EFTS had moved in with the statutory Tiger Moth from Hamble, forced by the German onslaught on Britain to move to quieter climes. The same applied to Nos 4 and 11 Air Observer and Navigator Schools who flew

170

their Ansons into Watchfield from Ansty and Hamble respectively. It had been intended all along that Watchfield was to be purely a training airfield and with aircraft such as Tiger Moths and Ansons flying around the circuit all day, it certainly became one of the busiest in the county. Far from the Battle of Britain raging over the coastal counties, the job of training could continue uninterrupted.

In October, No 1 Blind Approach School formed at Watchfield. It was operated initially by a civilian company named Air Service Training who were a subsidiary of Hawker Siddeley. Flying four Ansons, these were supplemented by three Link Trainers. Although not fully intended for blind approach training, this first electrical-mechanical flight simulator was a good platform to practise the art. Invented in 1920 by an American, Edward Albert Link, for obvious reasons it became known as the Link Trainer and was a basic set-up of an aircraft cockpit complete with instruments. It was able to move from side to side, up and down and round and round to simulate an aircraft's movements, all of which were recorded on a separate consul. From this humble beginning came the sophisticated aircraft simulators of today.

With a change of name to the Blind Approach Training Development Unit, this was changed later to the Wireless Intelligence Development Unit. The new title reflected the research and investigation that was going on into the Luftwaffe's use of wireless beams for target finding and appeared to take priority over the blind approach training. Nonetheless, a further two Ansons arrived at Watchfield and were equipped with blind approach equipment already being used at Boscombe Down, the RAF experimental establishment.

Watchfield now became a very busy station. The circuit was never clear of the Tiger Moths of No 3 EFTS or the Ansons of No 1 BAS. Work was also in progress on installing a Standard Beam Approach Aid at the airfield. A German invention produced by G. Lorenz AG and Telefunken, by 1935 it was in regular use in Germany, test flights having been carried out by the national airline, Lufthansa. The equipment used at Watchfield had been snatched from Holland before the invasion of that country and was put to good use in the early instruction of blind approach training.

The first two week course began on 28th October 1940 when six pupils arrived. Their training began in the Link Trainer and was followed by 12 hours' flying instruction. Other courses followed over the winter period and were only interrupted early in 1941 when the enemy strayed a long way inland and found Watchfield.

The incident occurred on Wednesday, 27th February 1941. Though a cloudy day, the visibility was moderate, this encouraging daylight activity by the enemy over much of Southern England and South Wales. One of the principal targets was London with the attack commencing between 19.35 and 22.30 hours. This particular attack was marred by thick mist, leaving much of the bombing to be done by radio navigation. One particular aircraft travelled past the capital to find an airfield below him and, not wanting to take his bombs home, dropped them on Watchfield. Five HE bombs together with further incendiaries were dropped along the boundary of the airfield. Although damage was done to the landing area, this was soon repaired enabling training to continue without mishap.

By 1941, the Standard Beam Approach Aid had been fitted to many military airfields. Maintenance of the system demanded constant calibration and in order to carry out such work, a further flight was formed at Watchfield. Given the title 'The Blind Approach Calibration Flight', it was equipped with, amongst others, two Airspeed Oxfords. The Oxford became the workhorse of the training and special flight units and was not finally withdrawn from RAF service until 1954. At Watchfield, three more were to join the flight later making the base very busy. This increase in units was facilitated by the Air Observer

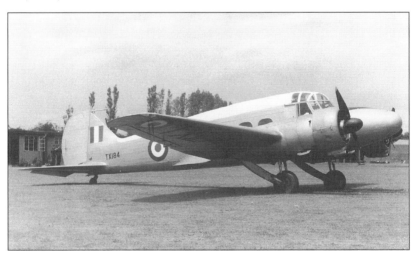

The Avro Anson was also the workhorse of all Oxfordshire bases and was known as the 'Faithful Annie'. This is the C-19 mark. (MAP)

and Navigator Schools, Nos 4 and 11, disbanding in the summer of 1941.

A change of aircraft from Anson to Oxford for No 1 Blind Approach School took place in September. At the same time plans were put forward to increase the number of pilots passing through the school to 1,100 per year. In addition, night flying was now encompassed within the school curriculum and any fine night would find the Oxfords airborne, sometimes to the consternation of the local populace. The introduction of a 24 hour flying schedule further agitated the situation but was found necessary in order to improve pilot output. In October 1941, the name was changed to No 1 Beam Approach School, this to remain for some considerable time. December of the same year saw the School of Flying Control form from Regional Control School, formerly at Brasenose College, Oxford. The unit provided air traffic control training with Ansons.

For a busy station, there had been relatively few accidents. Minor mishaps did occur from time to time, but the first serious incident did sadly end in a death. It happened during the particularly cold and snowy February of 1942. Oxford AT775 had taken off from Watchfield to carry out a series of blind flying tests. As the aircraft, flown by Sgt C. Rustron, turned downwind to land, a snowstorm blew up increasing the ice forming on the leading edge of the wings and completely obscuring the pilot's vision. Attempting to land blind, the aircraft went into a stall from which it never recovered. From around 15 feet, it smashed into the landing area, killing the pilot. It was a sad day for Watchfield.

Further aircraft were moved into the School of Flying Control in the shape of four De Havilland Dominies. A five or six seat navigational trainer or a ten seat communications aircraft, they were of wooden construction with fabric covering. The type gave excellent service throughout and beyond the war and even today, many examples are still flying. Allocated to No 1 BAS, they were primarily used for giving the SFC pupils experience of actual flights and aircraft. The addition of extra aircraft and extra flying forced the base to look for a satellite airfield. They found Kelmscot, which came into use on 17th October 1942.

Throughout the winter and into the spring of 1943, very little changed at Watchfield. The Oxfords of the Calibration Flight had moved over to Bicester during July 1942 but with such a throughput of pilots, another flight was added to the BAS enabling around 1,450 to

Very welcome at all airfields, the NAAFI wagon. This mobile unit is seen getting the

usual reception. (SE Newspapers)

pass through the school each year. Being a training base, operational aircraft were warned not to fly near or attempt to land at Watchfield.

A second satellite, Wanborough, came into use during July 1943 and a 'Q' site was established at Kingston Warren. This was a night decoy built on derelict land so as to avoid injury or death to civilians. It was equipped with a dummy 'Drem' lighting system and means of simulating aircraft movements on the ground. It was the ultimate deception to get the enemy to drop his bombs on the decoys but with Oxfordshire being far from the front line, its use was never really exploited.

Training continued unabated throughout 1943 with the Beam Approach Technical Training School moving over to Cranwell as the year drew to a close. The Beam Approach Development Unit had moved to Hinton-in-the-Hedges in April.

The Christmas period saw much talk about an invasion upon the Continent during 1944 and as if to emphasise the fact, a series of transport aircraft began to use Watchfield. Some were towing gliders whilst others were singletons but carrying troops. This practice continued until after D-Day, but Watchfield still went on with its training duties.

The next few years saw very little change until No 1 BAS disbanded on 31st December 1946. During its six years of existence, the school's aircraft had flown 100,000 hours with some 8,500 pupils passing through the school. All of this with just one accident involving injury.

The peacetime years saw the main unit renamed the School of Air Traffic Control during 1946. They stayed until 1950, after which the airfield became vacant and was used for parachute dropping with troops and aircraft from nearby Brize Norton.

Today's pilots have much to thank those who worked at Watchfield for, and those at Farnborough and Boscombe Down who worked on the development of Blind Approach. It was in those dark days of 1940 that this system was in its infancy and it is thanks to those early scientists and trainee pilots that we have the safety that we enjoy today.

15
WESTON-ON-THE-GREEN

The first nation to realise the potential of using towed gliders to convey troops and equipment to a combat area was Russia. They began to develop parachuting and gliding soon after the First World War and by 1935, had an elite corps of men ready to be carried in gliders. The Polish army were the next to recognise the use of such a force, followed by the French. For the Germans, bound by the terms of the 1919 Treaty of Versailles, the task of forming such units could not be seen publicly to be happening. Sport parachuting and gliding, however, had no such restrictions and behind this innocent facade was created an army of ready trained troops. When in 1935, Hitler announced that Germany no longer recognised the validity of the treaty, thousands of ready-trained troops joined the parachute regiments whilst other trained glider pilots joined the Luftwaffe.

For England, 22nd June 1940 became a day for the history books. It was on this day that Winston Churchill ordered that a force of 5,000 British airborne troops was to be formed and trained accompanied by the formation and training of a glider regiment for transporting them to the battlefields.

Long before this however, in 1931, a young woman aided by two RAF officers, had designed a towed glider capable of carrying cargo. The specially built glider was air-towed from Manston in Kent to Reading on 20th June 1931, where it landed to deliver mail. Despite the success, the aero-towing of gliders was considered dangerous and was banned in Britain. Sadly, the woman designer had to resign herself to the fact that Britain was not yet ready to accept this mode of travel and so she turned to writing romantic novels. Her name was Barbara Cartland. The resurgence of the idea in 1940 was implemented immediately and one of the sites chosen to train glider pilots was Weston-on-the-Green.

First acquired for military use in 1916, No 28 Training Depot Station was established at Weston on 27th July 1918. Sopwith Camels and Salamanders, and Avro 504s used it before closure in 1921. It returned to agriculture until the signs of another war became imminent whereupon it became a satellite of Brize Norton. The day before war broke out, No 90 Squadron brought their Blenheim IVs to Weston from Bircham Newton. They left for West Raynham four days later, returning to Weston on 14th September for two days. It was further used by Ansons and Blenheims from Bicester until No 13 OTU formed in April 1940.

Though just a satellite airfield, Weston was subjected to several enemy attacks during the Battle of Britain. The first came on Friday, 9th August 1940 which for the Luftwaffe was a quiet day with just isolated raids being carried out. Though cloudy over the Channel, several aircraft crossed the coast and approached Sunderland, causing some damage to the shipyards. When darkness fell, enemy aircraft once again crossed the East Coast and headed for Broadchalk in Wiltshire. Returning from the initial target, one of the aircraft dropped 16 HE bombs in a two mile line, some of them falling on Weston. Damage was done to the landing area and surrounding dispersals but nothing too serious. The Luftwaffe returned on the night of 25th/26th August when a bunch of incendiaries were dropped. As a follow up, the next evening Luftflotte 2 and 3 were active in the Midlands and once again found Weston on the way home. Though a very insignificant airfield at this period of the war, it had already received more bombs in weeks than any other Oxfordshire airfield had throughout the entire war. This very unwelcome attention was to last into September, luckily with very little serious damage or loss of life.

No 13 OTU continued their stay at Weston throughout the summer but by November 1940 they had left and the station became an RLG for No 15 SFTS based at Kidlington. Regular users were Harvards and Oxfords of the unit, so much so that by February 1941, it was felt necessary to base a detachment of groundcrew permanently at the base for the purpose of refuelling and repair work.

The rest of 1941 continued in a similar vein with just one incident worthy of mention. For some time around this period, it had been known that German aircraft were coming over at night with the sole intention of attacking training units carrying out night flying. Such an occasion came to Weston on 12th August 1941 when with good moonlight, the Oxfords were practising night take-offs and landings with trainee crews. Unknown to them, an enemy aircraft had infiltrated the circuit and after an abortive attempt to shoot down one of the Oxfords, had found Oxford W6629. It was a direct hit on the fuel tanks and the aircraft promptly burst into flames and crashed a short distance from the airfield, killing Norwegian F/Sgt Julin-Olsene and LAC C. P. Blair. The enemy further caused havoc by dropping six bombs on the airfield and strafing seven Oxfords on the ground. It was the worst attack on Weston yet.

By now Weston had been earmarked as a future glider training base. December 1941 saw No 15 SFTS close at Weston and Kidlington and No 2 GTS, affiliated to No 1 GTS at nearby Thame, was formed. However, the start of training was held back by a shortage of instructors and training gliders plus the aircraft to tow them. Eventually several General Aircraft Hotspur gliders were made available together with Hawker Hectors to tow them and training was able to start.

It is interesting to note that at this time, the obsolete biplane Hector had been given a new lease of life as a tug. Dating back to 1933, they were intended for Army Co-Operation use, but were soon replaced by the monoplane Westland Lysander. The GAL 48 Hotspur glider on the other hand was designed as a combat glider but never performed in this role. Designed to accommodate eight fully armed troops and with the ability to carry cargo, it was later found that from a military capability view, it was far better to have a larger glider that would accommodate 25 troops thus requiring fewer aircraft and lessening the risk of accidents when flying in large formations.

With a complement of eight Hectors and several Hotspurs, the first trainees arrived to find an airfield which was often unusable due to the bad drainage of the landing area. The Hectors were also found to be lacking in performance and thoughts were turned to a change of aircraft. A Fairey Battle was tested and found to be unsuitable but trials with a Hawker Audax, the Army Co-Op version of the delightful Hart, proved that in the role of glider tug, it was very suitable.

Accommodation for the aircraft arrived in the form of a twelve-bay Bessoneau hangar together with two more Over Type Blister hangars. With the first six-week glider pilots' course commencing on 2nd

179

GAL Hotspur gliders together with a Hawker Audax tug aircraft and an Avro Anson

January 1942, five more Audaxes arrived on 7th March.

It had been agreed back in 1941 between the Air Ministry and the War Office that the responsibility for airborne operations must be a Royal Air Force one. However, a prior policy dated September 1940 stated that the personnel to be trained to fly the gliders would be obtained from the army. This became a bone of contention between the Air Ministry and War Office for many years and many hundreds of minutes of meetings were heated in the extreme! The final word at that time was given by the then Deputy Chief of Air Staff, 'Bomber' Harris. He declared that using army personnel was wrong and the gliders should be flown by RAF bomber pilots.

This ruling stood until 1941 when a change of policy dictated that

at Weston-on-the-Green, June 1942. (Crown via Air Britain)

RAF pilots were needed elsewhere and could not be spared for glider pilot training. On 29th September 1941, the Army Council agreed that men could be taken from the ranks for glider pilot training. Over 5,000 army men had already applied for transfer to the RAF for aircrew duties and the personnel for training were drawn from these. All the RAF pilots who were already being instructed on gliders were returned to normal RAF duties by October 1942 but they continued to fly the tug aircraft.

As with any training there was always an element of danger. Several serious accidents occurred during these early months, none of them luckily causing loss of life. With the addition of night flying, the Hawker biplanes were found to be hopelessly inadequate and a search began once again for a replacement tug. Various aircraft were tested

181

including a twin-engined Oxford, but the final choice came down to the Miles Master II. Developed from the Miles Kestrel trainer, it was to succeed that type in the same role but somehow got a cool reception in military circles when it failed to meet specification T.6/36 required by the Air Ministry. Despite this, 3,301 Masters were produced, a lot of them being adapted for glider towing. In comparison with the Hector and Audax, it was a purpose-built aircraft.

By August 1942, Weston was indeed very busy accommodating 40 tug aircraft and a dozen Hotspurs. In good weather it was now possible to get 80 tows before dusk set in. With this increase in both gliders, tugs and courses, accidents, although few for the intense activity, were bound to happen. One such case was on 2nd September 1942 when Miles Master DL425 was towing Hotspur HH518. Lifting off successfully, it appeared as though the two aircraft were having trouble in gaining height. With its engine on full power, the Master clipped the steeple of Witney's church and fell to the ground. The glider pilot, having successfully released the tow cable, was able to land safely in a nearby field. Sadly the crew of the Master, Sgt Crouch and LAC Rodger, were killed. (See the Civilians at War chapter.)

Glider training continued into 1943 but with the onset of a particularly wet period, Weston became very waterlogged and for a period, No 2 GTS was detached to Cheddington to continue training. It had been decided to lay Sommerfeld Tracking on the landing area and perimeter track whilst the unit was away. This was not done until September but No 2 GTS returned regardless to Weston on 20th March 1943.

It was at this time that it had been decided that all glider training would now come under a new label. Consequently all the Glider Training Schools ceased to be such and became Pilots Advanced Flying Units or (P)AFU for short. No 2 GTS at Weston became No 20 (P)AFU on 6th April 1943 and once again Weston became a satellite airfield of Kidlington. Most of these units had been allocated the Airspeed Oxford, 36 of which now arrived at Weston. It became very necessary to lay Sommerfeld Track with the larger aircraft churning up the grass and this was duly done in September 1943. Weston was now able to operate both day and night, much to the consternation of the locals.

Throughout 1943 and 1944 intense flying training with Oxfords slotted in with the training of glider pilots continued but with the 1944 landings of D-Day and Arnhem a success, the pressure was relaxed a little. Disbandment of No 20 (P)AFU came as the final countdown to victory began in May 1945. Weston-on-the-Green remained in No 23 Group until 1st October 1945 when it was allocated to No 3 MU. On 15th March 1946 control of the airfield was passed to Upper Heyford. With the arrival of No 1 Parachute Training School at Heyford, the airfield was designated a dropping zone for parachutists under training, a role that continues today with the school at Brize Norton. A resurgence of importance came with the Korean War in the 1950s when the airfield was placed at the disposal of Bomber Command, and with the arrival of the Air Positioning Plotting Unit. They remained until 1951 when Weston was placed under Care and Maintenance.

It was not long, however, before it came once again into the fold of Training Command and became the major parachute dropping airfield in Oxfordshire. It retains this important function and is also a very active military and civilian gliding centre. Weston-on-the-Green looks set to continue in this role for many more years.

16
WITNEY

Though perhaps better known for its manufacture of high class blankets, the town of Witney and its airfield did much to aid the war effort. Completed during the First World War, the airfield was built by labour gangs consisting of German POWs and Portuguese labourers. On 30th March 1918, No 8 Training Squadron arrived to find a partially completed airfield. Avro 504Ks, F2Bs and DH5s were their main equipment and when they were joined by No 7 Training Squadron to form No 33 Training Depot Station, Witney became an important training station. The armistice however brought a quick end to military training and the unit disbanded in 1919.

The field once again became grazing pasture for cattle. Five of the six hangars erected for the training depot were quickly dismantled and sold. The landing area was marked out as tennis courts for the local club which remained in situ until 1928. With a renewed interest in civil flying, Universal Flying Services moved in and established a training school. Three aircraft, a Bristol Fighter, an Avro 504K and a DH60 'Moth', were used for flying instruction during the week and five shilling joyrides at the weekends.

A flying training school, Witney Aeronautical College, was established and joined with the Universal Flying Services who ran the Witney and Oxford Flying Club. As news spread regarding the new airfield, several owners of private aircraft decided to keep them on the site, ensuring a rapid expansion of flying activities at Witney.

The period between the two world wars was one that produced many new aircraft designs. With the rapid interest in air travel, there was certainly no shortage of aircraft designers all wanting to increase public awareness that it was quicker and safer by air. With the first attempt at a delta wing aircraft being made in 1930, it fell to Witney to see the concept fulfilled. *The Times* newspaper of Wednesday, 3rd August 1938 reported that a small aeroplane, the Delta Wing 9G, had been built to demonstrate that the design was practical, at Witney aerodrome in Oxfordshire. Designed and built by Mr P. Nesbitt-Willoughby, it was a totally experimental aircraft which got its name from its similarity in plan view to a capital delta, in the Greek alphabet. Unusual side wings had been incorporated that supplemented the tail booms.

Whilst all this was going on, Universal Aircraft Services had gone into liquidation by 1938 and the airfield was taken over by Witney Aerodrome Ltd. Life still carried on much the same with the addition of a branch of the Civil Air Guard becoming established, eventually training over 100 pilots.

As the war approached, the time available for test flying the Willoughby Delta became limited. During the summer of 1939, it flew continually on tests including one particular day, 7th July, which was to end in tragedy. Piloted by the Chief Flying Instructor, Mr Olly with Mr Willoughby as the passenger, it took off for a final flight late in the

The Willoughby Delta 9G with its designer and owner P. Nesbitt-Willoughby seen at Witney in 1939. (Aeroplane)

afternoon intending to just fly a few circuits and land. Somehow the pilot got lost, with reports of the aircraft being seen over Upper Heyford, ten miles away. Whilst approaching the airfield at Upper Heyford, it crashed into a field killing both men. The remains of the Willoughby Delta 9G were brought back to Witney but no satisfactory reason for the accident was ever found and with the war approaching, all thoughts of carrying on with the project foundered.

The advent of the war brought an end to civil flying in the country and in October 1939, the De Havilland Aircraft Company became sub-lessors of Witney as the airfield entered its most important stage. The service and spares department of De Havilland had been operating quite happily from Hatfield Airfield in Hertfordshire for many years. That is, until the war came and orders were received that no civil aircraft could operate east of a line drawn from Southampton to Edinburgh. Hatfield being within this 'no fly' zone, De Havilland were forced to look elsewhere for an airfield in which to establish their facility.

They found Witney and in early September 1939, Philip Gordon-Marshall, the manager of the Hatfield factory, made a quick aerial

The construction begins at Witney. Philip Gordon-Marshall beside a Tiger Moth. Also seen are a Rapide and a Miles Magister. (Flt Lt R. Jones)

186

Witney aerodrome when used by De Havilland. (Flt Lt R. Jones)

reconnaissance. Reporting that it looked satisfactory, the necessary arrangements were made with the Air Ministry who requisitioned the airfield on 27th September 1939. By October, some of the engineers from Hatfield had moved to the new site managing to live either in the little mess building on site or at one of the many farms nearby. Once settled in, the repair work began immediately on Queen Bee aircraft (remotely controlled Tiger Moths) and many other De Havilland types. Military-wise, Witney came under the umbrella of Brize Norton who used it as a RLG for the Oxfords of No 2 SFTS for a short period.

That winter the intense cold showed up many flaws after the comparative comfort of Hatfield. The heating proved inadequate, the hangar was draughty, and the men were thoroughly fed-up. Despite these hardships, work continued on maintaining the Queen Bees, used for Ack-Ack practise, and the twin-engined biplane Dominie. The latter were operated under the National Air Communications scheme but a change of policy created the Civilian Repair Organisation, part of which the De Havilland facility eventually became.

With the new organisation and the ever increasing number of aircraft

A Dominie, the military version of the Rapide, awaits collection. Seen left to right are Mr Thorn of De Havilland, Wg Cdr Davidson (Danish Air Force) and Flt Lt Jones. (Flt Lt R. Jones)

arriving at Witney, it was decided to build two new Bellman hangars. These were soon filled with Tiger Moths in different stages of crash damage having been sent from the many flying training schools now established throughout the country. The Dominies and Rapides that arrived were converted for two entirely different purposes. In the case of the Dominies, they were mainly being made into six-seat wireless trainers, with just a handful converting to airborne ambulances. The Rapides, however, were destined for places such as Turkey, India, Iceland and Southern Rhodesia. Then, with the fall of Dunkirk and the end of the Phoney War, the work of De Havilland took on a new purpose.

In June 1941, the first Hawker Hurricane flew in for repair. Within one week it was followed by four more and as the pace for repairs rapidly quickened, so the hunt for more space was accelerated. Daily it was the task of Mr Gordon-Marshall to look for suitable premises that could be adapted to serve as workshops. Even the many cattle byres and pig barns within the area came under his scrutiny and some came very close to being chosen! Eventually it was the more obvious places that were requisitioned – the Blarney Garage, standing close to the main gate of the airfield, Town Hill Garage and Haines Repair Workshop. Dents Glove Factory in nearby Charlbury became the main repair shop for the recovering of fabric components such as Tiger Moth wings. All of these served their purpose admirably and had the Luftwaffe attacked in force and destroyed the airfield, plans had already been formalised to move everything to these locations and continue the work.

With the very real threat of an invasion came the question of airfield defence and security. A branch of the Home Guard consisting of De Havilland employees was formed and carried out the night patrols of the site. This was in fact a unique Home Guard platoon in that it was of such importance as to warrant being commanded by a regular serving army officer. In later years the job of airfield defence was handed over to the RAF Regiment but throughout 1940 and 1941, the De Havilland Home Guard were ready to repel any would-be invader. Had the unthinkable happened, the night superintendent had orders to blow up

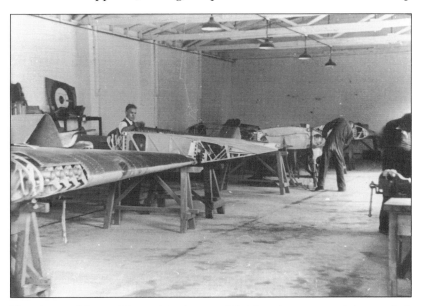

The wing workshop at Witney. Hurricane and Spitfire wings are seen being repaired. (Flt Lt R. Jones)

parts of the factory lest it fell into the enemy's hands.

With the increase in Hurricane repairs, it was found necessary to transfer the Tiger Moth work to the Auster Aircraft Company. At around the same time, Brush Electrical had been given a contract to build Dominies, a significant part being played by the Witney factory in securing the outcome. This allowed De Havilland to concentrate fully on fighter aircraft which, with the shortage of aircraft becoming a problem for Fighter Command at this stage of the war, ensured that they were back in squadron service as quickly as possible. In order to accommodate all the extra work, the two new Bellman hangars were cleared of stores to allow the Hurricane work to be carried out in relative comfort.

This upsurge in use brought its own problems, not the least being the fact that Witney airfield was not connected to the main electricity supply. Power therefore had to be generated on site by a diesel engine-driven generator which could only just produce enough electricity for the hangar and the administration buildings. With all the other buildings also requiring power, the system frequently overloaded causing untold problems. This continued for some time until finally the airfield was connected to the main electricity supply.

When the aircraft arrived at the airfield to be repaired or overhauled, their guns were unloaded and taken off by RAF personnel before the planes were taken to the Survey hangar for dismantling and cleaning prior to inspection. Processing the aircraft in Survey meant giving instructions for sufficient dismantling of the structure and systems to allow assessment of the damage, inspecting every dismantled part thoroughly and producing a full repair report stating what needed to be done, including a list of the parts that required replacement.

The most difficult to assess and repair were the Sea Hurricanes. These were Hurricanes specially adapted to be launched from a catapult mounted on the front deck of a small cargo ship. They were widely used both in the battle of the Atlantic and on the Russian convoys to Murmansk. These aircraft were always badly affected by corrosion and it was the job of Survey to assess if a component was too corroded to repair. The team were able to process one Hurricane a day. To begin with it took several weeks to repair and overhaul an aircraft but by the end of the war, the factory could return one fighter to service every working day.

With the job of repairing the damaged aircraft completed, it fell to the test pilot to carry out the ground running and air test. This task was

PRODUTION SPITFIRE TEST

Aircraft
No...... *EN H9L* .... Type.. *VII* ..... Engine. *64* ....

Airscrew..... *RJ7J7.* ....

Date	Pilot	Time Up	Down	Remarks
3/36	*B*			*Spray RPM ± 4wL3 BD*

Take off :- MB Reading ... *998* .... R.P.M. *3000* ....
-470/5 Boost... *+12* .... I.A.S... *95* ....

Observations on Climb (Alt. Set to 1013.5 MBS)

Indic. Height	R.P.M.	Boost	I.A.S.	Cab.Alt. Press.	Oil Press.	Temp.	Cool-ant.
6000	*2850*	*+12*	*176*		*95*	*52*	*95*
12,000	*2850*	*+12*	*170*				
14,000		*+12*	*170*				
LEVEL SPEED *10,000*			*15*				

Functioning of:-

Pilots seat control. *✓* ... Cold/warm air control ......
Radiator control *✓* ..... Air compressor ....
Brakes . *✓* .... Instruments ....
Chassis... *✓* .... Voltage ....
Ailerons... *✓* ....Thermostat................
Trimmers... *✓* .... Flaps ....
Fuel system.. *✓* .... Oleos.................
Mixture .... Landing Lamps.............
Coupe ....Deck arrester gear..........

Witney Spitfire production sheet – each aircraft had its own history recorded.

Pilot Officer Richard Jones of Duxford's No 19 Squadron pictured in his Spitfire during the Battle of Britain. He later became chief test pilot for De Havilland at Witney with the rank of Fl Lt. (Imperial War Museum – ref. CH1462)

initially done by the manager, Philip Gordon-Marshall, until he was joined by a serving RAF officer seconded to De Havilland. Flt Lt Richard Jones had served with distinction during the Battle of Britain. For ten months during this period he had flown in Nos 19 and 64 Squadrons from such famous fighter airfields as Kenley, Hornchurch, Hawkinge, Duxford and Rochford. Taken off operations in April 1941 and seconded to the Ministry of Aircraft Production, he was lent to the De Havilland Aircraft Co as test pilot to the Witney factory. Richard was in fact the only RAF member amongst the many civilians employed at the site. Now he was to carry out test flying on the types of aircraft that he had been flying during the battle.

It says much for the piloting skills of both Richard and Philip that despite the distinct dip in the middle of the grass airfield, no aircraft crashed at Witney during the war although there were a few hair-raising incidents when the Air Transport Auxiliary DH89, transporting the women pilots to fly the repaired fighters back to the squadrons, suddenly ran out of grass and, braking heavily, would tip onto its nose. Luckily the only damage done by that was to the propeller.

It cannot be emphasised enough that the work carried out at Witney could not have reached its level of expertise and professionalism without the employment of many women. They worked alongside the men in all sections and departments, overhauling engines, electrical installations, hydraulics, air frames etc. They also acted as inspectors and charge-hands as well as in the then more usual jobs of administration, cooking and nursing. Without their excellent and dedicated work in difficult conditions together with very long hours, the factory would certainly never have been able to play its vital role in the war effort.

During 1942, the repairing of Hurricanes began to dwindle only to be replaced by an ever increasing number of Spitfires requiring attention. One occasion connected with the Hurricanes must however be recorded as one of Witney's finest moments. It was Easter 1942 and the workforce were all looking forward to a few days leave. During the week prior to Easter, orders were received that a considerable supply of spare parts were needed for Hurricanes that were being sent to

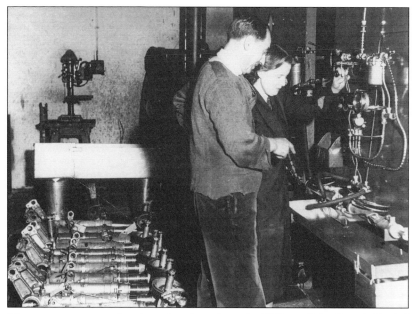

Many women were employed on aircraft repair work at Witney. (John Dossett-Davies)

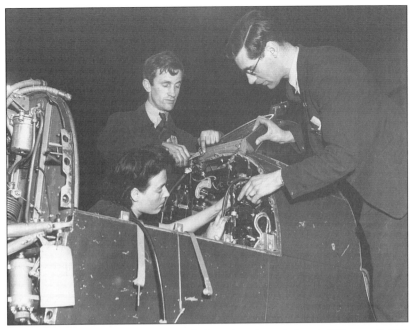

Women are given instruction on refitting aircraft cockpits at Witney. (British Aerospace via John Dossett-Davies)

Russia. The only way to obtain them was for Hurricanes to be flown to Witney and stripped of the required parts, which then had to be overhauled and cleaned and packed ready for shipment.

Such was the urgency of the job that it meant continuous working for the Witney workforce through the entire Easter period. Nineteen Hurricanes were flown in late on the Thursday before Good Friday. They were dismantled, cleaned, overhauled, crated and packed and the parts were dispatched to Russia by the end of the Easter Monday. Some men worked the day shift and round the clock on the following night shift, went home for two to three hours, then returned and worked the second day shift without any real sleep. So quickly was this accomplished that the workers went forward to meet the planes as they taxied in. So keen were the workers that the Squadron Leader's aircraft which he was due to fly back to his squadron later in the day, was partially dismantled whilst he was taking a cup of tea in the canteen!

By the end of the year, both Bellman hangars had been turned over to Spitfire work with the original No 1 Hangar still being used for work on De Havilland aircraft. Delivery of repaired aircraft back to the squadrons was still being carried out by the Air Transport Auxiliary whose one complaint about Witney was that it was so well camouflaged that it was difficult to find when they came in on the ferry aircraft. The complaints became so many that De Havilland were officially instructed to put out boundary markers to make the airfield easier to locate. This very effective camouflage may well be the reason that Witney was only once the subject of a Luftwaffe attack. This was on 22nd November 1940 when two bombs were dropped, both missing the works and the airfield completely although 200 houses were damaged outside the boundary.

The repair of Hurricanes and Spitfires continued at Witney until 1945 when, with the war at an end, the decision was made to once again concentrate on pure De Havilland aircraft. Accordingly, 108 RAF Dominies were converted into civil passenger aircraft whilst Mosquitos were being refurbished and sold to other countries. The new De Havilland Dove, a twin-engined transport aircraft, also used the

A typical scene at Witney. With the now camouflaged hangars are Hurricanes, Spitfires and Rapides (note the American Spitfire second from right). (Flt Lt R. Jones)

Witney airfield in 1941. The camouflage effect is seen to appear as several different fields. (John Dossett-Davies)

facilities for repair and servicing. These operations were to continue until August 1949 when notice was received to close the airfield with most of the staff being offered the chance to relocate to the De Havilland factory at Leavesden in Hertfordshire. In 1951, Smith Industries established a factory on the airfield using many of the old buildings but when they left, Witney fell into disrepair. It formed part of the Windrush Industrial Park but very little remains today as evidence of this great institution.

During the ten years of occupation, over 1,400 aircraft had been test flown from Witney. With the last Hurricane leaving on 26th October 1944 and the last Spitfire on 5th December 1945, the total number of aircraft returned to service was 373 Hurricanes and 396 Spitfires. These figures together with 803 various De Havilland aircraft add up to a very important part of Britain's war effort. In December 1943, Sir Stafford Cripps, then Minister of Aircraft Production, had told the Witney workers that 'no less than 40% of all aircraft going back into RAF service are reconditioned from repair units. Your work is of the utmost importance.' What went on at Witney was a magnificent achievement.

196

Presentation to Flt Lt Richard Jones (far left) at the end of test flying from Witney in 1945. Pictured far right is the general manager, Philip Gordon-Marshall. (Flt Lt R. Jones)

The final repaired Spitfire is handed over to the RAF in 1949. (John Dossett-Davies)

Flt Lt Richard Jones, De Havilland test pilot, with a non-fare paying passenger, in a Tiger Moth. The dog, Nichi, loved to fly. (Flt Lt R. Jones)

We cannot, however, leave this chapter without the mention of dogs. Many squadrons during the war had dogs as mascots but Witney had them as an integral part of the make-up of De Havilland. Aside from the Alsatians employed on security when the RAF Regiment took over the defence of Witney, there was 'Nichi'. He was a bulldog, the property of Philip Gordon-Marshall, the De Havilland manager, and a character in his own right. A popular photograph published in the *Field* of 25th September 1943 and accompanied by an article written by A. Croxton Smith OBE, showed Nichi in the front cockpit of a Tiger Moth about to be flown by test pilot, Flt Lt Jones. Apparently, the animal had acquired a taste for flying! He also managed to embroil himself in several incidents, one of which nearly proved fatal.

Being given the run of the airfield, he one day took exception to a turning propeller. Before anyone could stop him, Nichi attacked the blades, only to fall back with the right side of his head apparently torn off. As he lay still on the tarmac, some of the workers pronounced him dead and reverently, placed him in a barrow, covered him with a black sack and wheeled him away to await his master's return.

To the workers' amazement, 30 minutes later, Nichi was loping through one of the buildings with half his head hanging off to get to the office of Mr Gordon-Marshall and the one place where he knew he would get comfort. Nichi was rushed to the local vet who found, although he was badly wounded, that most of the damage had been done to all the loose skin around the head and the left eye and not the skull. Nichi was duly repaired with clips securing the broken skin and was chauffeured back to the airfield feeling very sorry for himself.

There it may have ended happily but no! Whilst being carried from the car to his master's office, Nichi espied with his one good eye, a Siamese cat accompanying a woman client. This was too much of an insult to bear and managing to escape from his carrier, he bore down upon the enemy with his surgical clips flying. Swiftly the pair were separated but not before Nichi had received several nasty scratches to his nose and good eye which warranted another visit to the vet to have these wounds treated and the clips replaced. Thereafter he was grounded in his master's office and, glad to say, made a full recovery, continuing to get into further trouble as well as taking up flying again!

With the end of the war and the eventual demise of Witney, it was

Philip Gordon-Marshall with his dog Nichi and a Tiger Moth, Witney 1941. (Flt Lt R. Jones)

said by a former Inspector and past chairman of the De Havilland Fellowship, John W. Dosset-Davies, that 'it was like the break-up of a large family'. The De Havilland spirit, as it became known, pervaded every section and every corner of Witney. This feeling must be rare but it conjures up a true picture of the camaraderie and hard work that was evident at this small Oxfordshire airfield.

17
THE OTHER
AIRFIELDS

There were numerous wartime airfields in Oxfordshire that do not warrant an entire chapter due to the fact that they were either operational for very short periods, were relief or satellite airfields, or were just used on occasions. This should in no way decry their value towards the war effort for without them, the major airfields may well have been overcrowded and thus reduced in effectiveness. Some signs of their existence remain today but many have faded into the agricultural background of the county. In their own way, they were all very important.

AKEMAN STREET
Developed in late 1939 as an RLG for No 2 SFTS at Brize Norton, it took its name from a Roman road that cut directly across the airfield. It was completed in July 1940, just in time for the Advanced Training Squadron of No 2 SFTS to move in after Brize Norton had been bombed by the Luftwaffe.

Although only a grass airfield, the Oxfords found little problem in using Akeman Street which for a change, had good drainage qualities. Three grass runways were laid out together with living quarters, mess buildings, air raid shelters and even a small operations room. Ten Over Type Blister hangars were erected together with one Bellman hangar. On 14th March 1942, No 2 SFTS was redesignated 2 (P)AFU but by July of that year the unit had ceased to exist. The Oxfords returned to Brize

Norton and the airfield was allocated to No 6 (P)AFU based at Little Rissington. Once again the Oxfords returned, this time until February 1947 when flying ceased completely and Akeman Street was left deserted.

CHIPPING NORTON

One of the larger RLGs or satellite airfields in the county was Chipping Norton. Situated two miles south of the village of that name, it was once again a Service Flying Training School that used the airfield first after its completion by 10th July 1940. Like so many others, it was a grass airfield with the usual three runway layout. The north-west/south-east was 1,000 yards, east/west was 800 yards and the north/south just 600 yards. Two Bellman hangars were constructed on the northern boundary with just one Over Type Blister hangar at the extreme end of the same boundary. Accommodation was in the style of Bell tents with a few wooden huts to act as stores etc.

The Airspeed Oxfords of the Advanced Training Squadron of No 15 SFTS were the first type to use the base, arriving on 10th July 1940. The same month they began to re-equip with the North American Harvard, one of the first American aircraft to be ordered by the RAF. This type remained the standard equipment for all flying training schools for over 16 years. Comprising an all-metal stressed-skin construction, its power plant was a huge radial Pratt and Whitney Wasp engine producing so much energy that at full power, the propeller tips went supersonic giving it a mighty roaring sound. Far noisier than the twin-engined Oxford, it did not endear itself to the Chipping Norton villagers!

In August 1940, No 15 SFTS was consolidated at Kidlington, but the Advanced Training Squadron remained at Chipping. Squadron strength now stood at 41 Harvards and 15 Oxfords as the airfield became an RLG for Kidlington. It came to the attention of the Luftwaffe over the night of Tuesday, 29th and Wednesday, 30th of October.

Designated as being the end of the Battle of Britain, it was a very busy October night with the enemy active over the country. Heavy raids were carried out on the Midlands as what seemed like a last convulsive spasm took place. Some of the Midlands raiders found Chipping Norton and dropped incendiary and high explosive bombs within the vicinity. No damage was done to the airfield but it did bring home that even training bases were not immune to attack. As if to emphasise the fact, the enemy once again attacked the airfield over the night of 18th/19th November 1940, this time dropping high explosive bombs on the landing area.

No 6 SFTS now used the airfield, once again with Oxfords, as big extensions took place with three Extra Over Type Blister hangars being built and Sommerfeld Tracking being laid on the two main runways. Like the majority of SFTSs, No 6 now changed to 6 (P)AFU on 1st April 1942. This unit was to remain at Chipping Norton until the end of the war, finally closing in December 1945. Many signs of its existence remain today.

COWLEY

Forever known as the home of Morris Motors, Cowley was also the base of No 1 Civilian Repair Unit. Officially opened on 11th September 1939, it had been repairing Hurricanes and Spitfires since early that year, collected from around the country by No 5 MU.

The unit had formed as a result of the boss of Morris Motors, William Morris later Lord Nuffield, setting up a private company to develop aero engines at his Wolseley plant as early as 1929. He had become convinced of the role that aircraft would play in the coming years, and at his suggestion, the RAF had handed over the job of repairing damaged aircraft to private industry. With Lord Nuffield becoming Director General of Maintenance, Cowley became the headquarters of the Civilian Repair Organisation as well as its No 1 depot. A new unit called No 1 Metal Produce and Recovery Depot was formed to recycle damaged and crashed aircraft and their components, eventually extending its premises to over 100 acres.

By the spring of 1940, when Lord Nuffield handed over control of the operation to the newly formed Ministry of Aircraft Production, the unit had five main repair centres served by a network of over 1,000 smaller repair units all over the country. The repair work was in addition to making radiators for Spitfire, Lancaster, Halifax and Mosquito aircraft. Their expertise in the field of radiators was sought by Vickers themselves when they were experiencing overheating problems with the Merlin engines in the Spitfires. The workforce, having lost the car production for the duration of the war, were indeed glad of this and the repair work.

Several flight test hangars and a grass landing ground had been constructed alongside the main factory. Some pilots, eager to get their aircraft repaired, would themselves fly their aircraft to Cowley if possible in order to save time. Bearing this in mind, it is interesting to

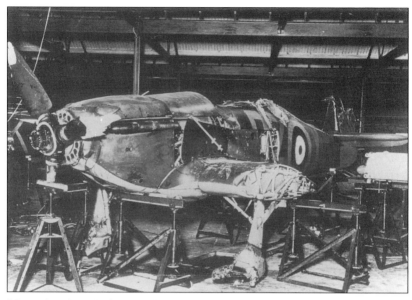

Many aircraft arrived at Cowley in an unrecognisable state, and (below) how the Hurricane looked after treatment.

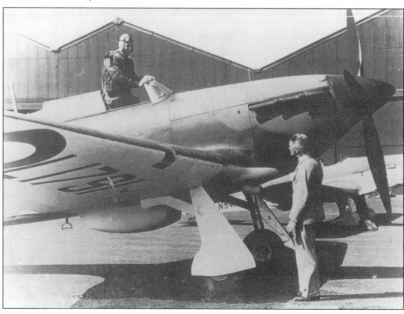

*A stalwart Tiger Moth, still flying in civilian hands, possibly built at Cowley.
(via A. Moor)*

note that of the total number of aircraft issued to fighter squadrons
during the Battle of Britain, only 65% were new aircraft straight from
the factory. The other 35% were reconditioned aircraft saved from the
scrap heap by units of the CRO.

Aircraft that were beyond repair at Cowley had every piece of alloy,
rubber and plastic taken from them for future use. From mid 1940
onwards, huge numbers of crashed aircraft, British and German, were
arriving at Cowley from all over the country and the piles of
accumulated salvage grew higher. As if to emphasis the importance
of spare parts for many aircraft, men from the Spitfire factory at
Southampton would come looking for spares. They not only visited the
established depots but any car junkyard within the area in the hope of
finding useful material. More men and women than ever before
became employed at the site, every one of them as well as the local
population as conscious as anybody of the dire consequences if the
RAF were to lose the Battle of Britain. Some of the workers were on
duty for 14 hours a day and seven days a week.

Until as late as 1945, Cowley was repairing damaged aircraft, but
this was not its only claim to fame. The factory also built 3,210 Tiger
Moths sub-contracted to them by De Havilland. This was a remarkable

achievement considering that the production in peacetime had been cars and not aircraft. It is fair to say that some Tiger Moths flying today, and there are many, may well have been built at Morris Motors at Cowley. The establishment's contribution to the Battle of Britain was very significant.

CULHAM

If your interest is in superbly preserved military buildings, then RNAS Culham is the place to see. The hangars, guard room, huts and shelters, though now in civilian use, bear witness to the many standard designs of military buildings emanating from the expansion period. Oddly though, RNAS Culham served during wartime for only a very short period.

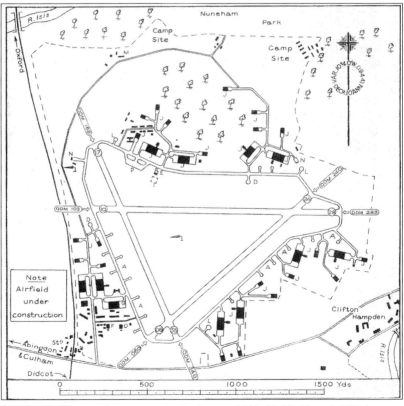

Wartime Culham, under construction in August 1944. (Public Record Office)

206

The Culham guardhouse, now a food store.

Commissioned as HMS *Hornbill* on 1st November 1944, it was an Aircraft Receipt and Despatch Unit. Very many types of aircraft used its facilities including Ansons, Fireflies, Reliants and Seafires, the naval version of the Spitfire. By 1945 the site was being run down but plans had already been made for Culham to become a peacetime naval base.

On 1st July 1947, No 1832 Squadron reformed as a fighter squadron in the RN Volunteer Reserve commanded by Lt Cdr P. Godfrey OBE, RNVR and drawing its personnel mainly from the Oxford and London areas. A nucleus of No 1832 formed No 1840 Squadron RNVR on 14th April 1951, who left for Ford in Sussex two months later. Two further units formed at Culham during 1952/3, these being Nos 1832A and 1832B, both moving over to Benson fairly quickly due to Culham being unsuitable for jet operations.

They were partnered by a Photographic Development Unit, No 739, equipped mainly with Sea Mosquitos and commanded by Lt (A) B. A. MacCaw DSC, RN. Part of the Central Photographic Establishment at Benson, they were forced to use Culham due to a shortage of hangar space at Benson. The unit, in addition to operating the Mosquito, also flew a Dominie, Anson, Sea Fury and a Sea Hornet for camera

Nissen huts abound at Culham.

installation and evaluation. No 739 Squadron disbanded at Culham on 12th July 1950.

HMS *Hornbill* was finally closed on 30th September 1953 but remained in Admiralty hands and was used as a store. The UK Atomic Energy Commission took over parts of the airfield during 1960 before more general industry moved in. Blister hangars, Pentad hangars, T2 hangars, all abound in plentiful supply at Culham for any historian to see.

ENSTONE

Opened as a second satellite for No 21 OTU at Moreton-in-the-Marsh near Gloucester on 15th September 1942, Enstone was not used until seven months later. Wellingtons of the OTU used the site until April 1944 together with the Flight (Gunnery) of the OTU who arrived on 17th May 1943. Although just a satellite airfield, 21 OTU used Enstone to carry out 'Nickelling' operations.

The Wellingtons of the OTU were partnered by a very 'hush-hush' unit about which very little has ever been known. It comprised six Avro Lancasters which, without any squadron markings or serial

208

numbers at all, were painted in a gloss black livery. They were kept away from the OTU and unless flying, out of sight of all other personnel. Heavily modified with the bomb doors removed, there is no official record of them being at Enstone over a period of 18 months. It has only recently been rumoured that they were being used for experiments in carrying the British atomic bomb which was in an advanced stage of production. As history records, the Americans were the only Allied power to drop the atomic bomb which they did on two occasions, both on Japan. Such was the secrecy surrounding the British development that until now, very few people knew of our involvement in an atomic bomb programme. Certainly, very little was known about the mysterious black Lancasters that resided at Enstone.

The crew of one of the mysterious black Lancasters based at Enstone. No markings were apparent on any of the aircraft. (Gordon Markham)

Rather unusually, Curtiss Tomahawks arrived at the base on 26th February 1944. The type was originally intended for the French but the collapse of France saw 140 of them taken into RAF service. Though intended as a low level tactical reconnaissance aircraft, the six that came to Enstone were employed in a training role. The Tomahawks were exchanged for Hurricanes before the flight was disbanded on 21st August 1944.

With victory, flying ceased at Enstone in November 1945 and it passed to Maintenance Command on 17th January 1946. In October it came under the control of Flying Training Command and a detachment of No 17 SFTS arrived with Harvards and Oxfords. By December 1946 they had moved on and Enstone was relegated to an RLG for Little Rissington near Gloucester. Today it is a civilian airfield operated by Glyme Valley Ltd and Enstone Aerocentre. Part of the 08/26 hard runway is still in use and the site is used by a mixture of aircraft including gliders and microlights. Some of the former RAF buildings are now used by industry.

GROVE

One of the large four-engined bombers that did not progress further than the prototype stage was the Vickers Windsor. A heavy bomber with an elliptical wing form, one of the prototypes, DW506, force-landed at Grove on 2nd March 1944 and was unfortunately written off at the airfield. It was a very ignominious end for what could have been a good bomber.

Classed as a spare bomber airfield for No 91 Group, August 1942 saw the Wellingtons of No 15 OTU make use of the site as Grove was transferred to Flying Training Command shortly after. Clearance of the site entailed removing a farmhouse and several outbuildings which were situated in the middle of the proposed airfield. The following year saw the Whitleys and Horsa gliders from Brize Norton using the field and in March 1943, Hurricanes of Nos 174 (Mauritius) and 184 Squadrons were at Grove for two days in connection with Operation 'Spartan'. At this time the numbers of personnel were minimal due to the fact that the accommodation was far from completed.

When they left it was the Oxfords of No 15 (P)AFU that used the airfield briefly for it had been earmarked for the Americans. The US 9th Army Air Force Command took control of Grove and used it as a repair and maintenance base for C-47 Dakotas and C-46 Commandos. It became known as 'Muddy Grove' as mud from the American lorries, which were continually being driven in and out of the construction area, was taken all through the village and deposited on the country lanes around the site.

Whilst the Americans were at Grove they brought in all their own equipment, furnishings, food etc which was shipped to England and then brought by lorry to the airfield. They were very generous to the locals, especially the young females, much to the consternation of the parents! As well as putting up their own accommodation on the airfield and in the village, they also built a ballroom and it was here that part of the Glenn Miller Band, a sextet led by Sgt Mel Powell, played on 12th August 1944 at a 9th Air Force Command dance.

The incident regarding the Vickers Windsor brought a temporary halt to operations but flying was to continue until February 1946 when the Americans left and Grove reverted back to RAF control. It was now used a an RLG but this was shortlived and by 1947, industry was seen to be encroaching on the airfield. Grove however, still holds a secret.

In the late 1970s, the Metal Box Company took over many of the buildings for their research and development complex. Since that time, many of the people working late have been subjected to a ghostly apparition. Late at night and in the early hours of the morning, a figure clothed in full flying gear has been seen. It moves slowly between the buildings before finally disappearing into thin air. The theory is that it is a crewman from a Lancaster bomber that crashed at Fyfield nearby. It was en route for bombing Germany when it developed engine trouble and attempted to land at Grove but it crashed and the bomb load exploded, killing all the crew. Local people are sure the old airfield site is haunted by the tragedy. A more tangible reminder of its past existence is a memorial placed at the entrance to the airfield which details the units that flew from Grove.

KELMSCOT

Acting as the RLG for Watchfield, Kelmscot came into operation on 17th October 1942. It was used by No 1 Beam Approach School, then resident at Watchfield, whose Oxfords practising blind approaches would land on the grass landing strip. It had just one Over Type Blister hangar and several huts. During May 1944 it became closed to flying and was used as a dropping zone for paratroops in preparation for D-Day. This period saw the most use of Kelmscot and although compared to other sites that may seem very little, it played its part in the preparation for the assault.

KIDDINGTON (GLYMPTON)

Opened in 1940, this was an RLG for the Harvards and Oxfords of No 15 SFTS. It was further used by gliders of the Kidlington OTU and by No 20 (P)AFU.

KINGSTON BAGPUIZE

For sheer nostalgia, this former RLG is certainly worth a visit. There in the middle of the airfield stands the control tower. Built to the specification 13726/41, it acts as a memorial to the airfield's former use.

Built on flat land to the south of the village, Kingston Bagpuize was operational by 1942 when No 3 EFTS used it as a RLG. It also served for a brief period as a satellite airfield for No 1 GTS then based at Thame. Between January and April of 1943, it was the gliders and tugs of No 4 GTS that could be seen in and around the circuit. On 10th March 1943, these were joined by the Oxfords of No 20 (P)AFU who used Kingston Bagpuize until July.

It was then that a period of expansion began as the USAAF took possession of the airfield. Fifty P-47 Thunderbolts arrived from the 368th Fighter Group at Greenham Common, not originally to operate from Kingston Bagpuize, but to test the durability of a wire mesh that

The magnificent tower still stands at Kingston Bagpuize.

had been laid on the grass. Once this was found to be substantial, the P-47s carried out several operations flying from the airfield before returning to Greenham Common. Trials on the wire mesh were carried out further by C-47s but in June 1944, the experimental surface was taken up and Kingston Bagpuize lay dormant. On 14th December 1944, No 3 MU began using the airfield, remaining until the site eventually closed on 14th June 1954. Industry has now taken over most of the wartime buildings with the exception of the control tower. Sitting there, very forlorn, it looks as though it is waiting for a ghost!

SHELLINGFORD
First introduced into service in February 1932, the De Havilland Tiger Moth was still in service with the RAFVR in 1951. No other aircraft can equal such a record and the type was a very familiar sight around Shellingford for many years.

For some time, No 3 EFTS had been looking for a suitable home after being forced to vacate Watchfield and finding Kelmscot unsuitable. They finally settled on Shellingford, situated four miles east of Faringdon. Tiger Moths of 'C' Flight were the first to arrive, the pupils finding the accommodation less than ideal. By December 1941 however, the situation had improved considerably and by then the

The workhorse of the Elementary Flying Training Schools, the Tiger Moth. Many are now in civilian hands. (via A. Moor)

213

56 remaining Tiger Moths of No 3 EFTS had moved fully to Shellingford.

The RLG at Kingston Bagpuize was soon active with the aircraft using it daily. Night flying had been introduced into the curriculum but Kingston was only available for a limited time and a search was made for another RLG. One suggestion was Wanborough but this was found to be unsuitable and in the end, Shellingford operated without a permanent RLG.

With the order that Army personnel were to be trained to fly gliders, the first arrived at Shellingford in July 1942. Flying training on the Moths and the gliders now increased dramatically and by March 1943, the flying hours had risen to 3,472.45, some 209 of them at night. Shellingford had a very peaceful war with the flying training continuing until 1945 and beyond. No 3 EFTS, together with Shellingford, closed on 31st March 1948.

STANTON HARCOURT

The official record for Friday, 16th August 1940 states that it was a mainly fair and warm day with Channel haze. It also tells us that airfields in Kent, Hampshire and West Sussex were attacked by the Luftwaffe. Other targets included Essex and Oxfordshire.

For the latter, it was late afternoon when several Ju 88s attacked Brize Norton with devastating results, but the satellite airfield at Stanton Harcourt was also hit. Still in the process of being built by Wimpey's, workmen were working on laying the hard runway when the Luftwaffe appeared overhead, strafing and bombing as they came in low. Five civilian workmen were killed instantly with another four later dying from their wounds. It was a devastating raid and together with the raid on Brize Norton, ranked as one of the worst attacks on an airfield in the county.

Work however had progressed sufficiently by 3rd September 1940 to allow No 10 OTU to commence using the base. The Whitleys of 'C' Flight moved in from Abingdon to concentrate on night flying training. Stanton Harcourt was the usual three runway layout with both T2 and B1 hangars, the latter needed to house the Whitleys and the later Halifax aircraft that were to use the base.

In 1940, the names of the German battleships *Scharnhorst* and *Gneisenau* were frequently in the press. The raiders were plundering Allied shipping to such an extent that it became a number one priority to attack and sink the ships, especially *Scharnhorst*. In 1941 came the news that both ships had put into the French port of Brest. The British public were confident that the RAF would attack and sink them. Many bomber squadrons were employed on the task including Nos 35 and 76 equipped with the Halifax. Both squadrons used Stanton Harcourt from which to mount their attacks on La Pallice, the hide-out for the German ships.

That the raids were carried out with great determination cannot be disputed, but it was not to be the end of the *Scharnhorst* or *Gneisenau*. Whilst the ships were hit several times, no serious damage was sustained. Further attacks brought the same result for the ships were too heavily protected and with netting and foliage camouflage, too difficult to pinpoint accurately from the air. The attacks, however, did ensure they stayed in harbour until February 1942, when the *Scharnhorst* and *Gneisenau* made their dash through the English Channel.

An unusual visitor to Stanton Harcourt in January 1943 was a Consolidated Liberator of Lyneham's No 511 Squadron. Serialised AL504 and named *Commando*, it carried Winston Churchill from Stanton Harcourt to the Casablanca conference.

The guard room and water tower, Stanton Harcourt. (Neil Richards)

215

One month later, the airfield was the home of A and D Conversion Flights of No 10 OTU. In the same year, Oxfords of No 1501 BAT Flight were to be seen frequently in the circuit and by March 1944, whilst new runways were laid at nearby Abingdon, the entire fleet of No 10 OTU was based at Stanton Harcourt. A change to Wellington Xs began in July 1944 but with the resurfacing at Abingdon complete, the OTU began to move there fully later in the year. By November 1945, Stanton Harcourt had become surplus to requirements and was closed.

WINDRUSH

Although now in the county of Gloucestershire, Windrush rests firmly on the borders of that county and Oxfordshire. Lying four miles west of Burford, and opened as an RLG for No 6 SFTS at Little Rissington in the summer of 1940, it is worthy of mention in this book due to the fact that an act of extreme heroism took place nearby.

The date was Sunday, 18th August 1940. Known in Battle of Britain annals as the 'hardest day', it was the South and the South Coast airfields that took the brunt of the many Luftwaffe attacks on that day. During the evening, further raids developed with some of the enemy

The memorial to a brave pilot at Windrush church. (Neil Richards)

aircraft straying inland. For the He 111s of the 2nd Gruppe of KG27 flying from Dinard it was the last raid of the day as they crossed the Channel at around 11.30 pm. One particular Heinkel (1408) had chanced to come across Windrush airfield, which was in the process of carrying out night flying exercises for No 6 FTS.

The grass runway at Windrush was lit by a crude form of lighting, aiding the several Anson aircraft that were doing circuits and bumps around the airfield. Managing to infiltrate the circuit, the He 111 followed an Anson that was turning to land. Dropping two 50kg HE bombs just short of the landing area, the enemy closed on the Anson (L9164), allowing the front gunner to fire in an attempt to shoot it down. The pilot of the Anson, Sgt B. Hancock, realising the position, turned off his navigation lights and banked hard to port. This action caused the He 111 to collide with the Anson, both aircraft crashing in a ball of fire two miles south-west of the landing ground at Blackbitch Farm, Aldsworth, Northleach. It was impossible for anyone to survive such a crash and sadly, Sgt Hancock and the crew of the Heinkel, Oberfw Dreher, Uffz Schmidt, Uffz Rave and Uffz Lohrs, were all killed instantly. It appeared at the time as though Sgt Hancock, realising that he was about to be shot down, deliberately turned into the path of the enemy, allowing the collision to happen and therefore saving other lives. His courage is recalled on a memorial plaque that is situated in the local churchyard at Windrush.

Always an RLG, Windrush was used by various SFTSs from both Oxfordshire and Gloucestershire. A few huts remain today, still a visible reminder, together with the plaque, of a very heroic episode in the life of a small landing ground.

OTHER SITES

EYNSHAM

A massive bomb dump serving Oxfordshire, up to 6,000 tons of explosives were held in the base at one time. Opened in 1939, it was first designated No 6 Air Ammunition Park with storage up to 1,000 tons, later renamed No 96 MU in October that year. It escaped devastation in February 1942 when a training aircraft crashed near the bomb store. The unit moved to Kidlington on 1st November 1948 and

Eynsham returned to civilian use. Some buildings remain today and are used for farm storage.

BARTON ABBEY

A little known satellite airstrip. No 28 Satellite Landing Ground opened on 30th September 1941 as a storage facility for No 8 MU at Little Rissington. This site is on the main Oxford to Banbury road at Hopcrofts Hall. Two Robin hangars were erected but the aircraft were dispersed into the trees for natural camouflage. The landing ground was assigned to No 39 MU at Colerne for six months from August 1942, reverting back to No 8 MU until it closed in February 1945. The types most commonly stored here were Wellingtons.

STARVEALL FARM

Another little known satellite airstrip. Known as No 2 Satellite Landing Ground, the airstrip opened on 1st July 1941 as a storage site for No 39 MU at Colerne, being reassigned to No 33 MU at Lyneham for five months from October 1941 and reverting to 39 MU until closure in September 1945. Amongst the many types stored here, Spitfires predominated.

WYKHAM HILL

Used by the Piper Cubs of the 696th Armoured Field Artillery Battalion, the unit was assigned to the 5th Field Artillery Group which had its headquarters at Banbury. The Cubs were used in the spotter role yet their activities do not feature in any US Army history. Arriving around 8th April 1944, they left Wykham Hill on 25th July 1944.

18
RAF MEDMENHAM

Less than one hour after the declaration of war, a Blenheim of Bomber Command took off from Wyton RAF base on the war's first official photographic sortie from Britain. It photographed the German fleet in Wilhelmshaven prior to an attack by Bomber Command. When the aircraft landed, the films were rushed to the Photographic Interpretation Unit at Wembley but when developed, it was found that the type of camera used lacked the clarity and definition required to assist Bomber Command. It was further found that the Blenheim was not the right aircraft for the job being somewhat slow and therefore prone to damage from enemy attacks and flak. As we have read in the Benson chapter, this first sortie gave way to the introduction of Sidney Cotton and his firm ideas on photographic reconnaissance which he presented to the Air Ministry.

It was early in 1941 that the PIU moved from Wembley to a safer and far more pleasant establishment. This was a large pseudo-tudor mansion called 'Danesfield' which looked southwards from a lovely site high above the River Thames between Marlow and Henley. When it was requisitioned by the RAF it became known as RAF Medmenham, the name taken from the little village nearby. It was left to Wg Cdr Peter Stewart, an officer in the auxiliary air force, to organise the expansion of the station, his first move being to militarize the unit. Some of the civilian personnel who had worked in Wembley had moved to Medmenham but this now meant that they would have to be in uniform.

The work of photographic interpretation got underway immediately. With the pilots of the PRU squadrons at Benson roaming far and wide and obtaining thousands of photographs, a system of successive stages of interpretation was introduced. Known as 'phases', the first meant immediate reporting of important news items such as the movement of

219

ships and aircraft together with rail and canal traffic. The second phase reports were to be out within 24 hours and concerned details of general activity, whilst the third phase to be issued was to contain detailed statements on such items as airfields, factories etc. It was however not only as an aid to targeting and damage assessment that the photographs were essential, it was also to find out what secret weapons the enemy possessed or was in the process of developing. One such was radar.

It was known by 1941 that the Germans had developed a new radio direction-finding apparatus. Photographs taken by Benson squadrons along a particular stretch of French coastline showed a house near the edge of the cliff at Bruneval. Sharp eyes at Medmenham, however, had spotted what looked like a paraboloidal installation. A further flight from Benson obtained close-up photos of the house at Bruneval and sure enough, it showed a German radar installation alongside. The clarity of the photographs was such that a raid on the area was immediately arranged and carried out with some success.

Perhaps, however, more well known was the discovery of the German 'V' weapon sites. For many months, photographs had been taken of Northern France, in particular an area known as Watten near

Tail view of one of the Mk II Spitfires of the PRU. (RAF Benson)

Calais. A clearing in a forest showed building activity culminating in a huge concrete dome structure. Rail line spurs were seen to be connecting further concrete structures whilst along the coastline of the Pas-de-Calais, strange ski-type structures began to appear on the photographs. Another area to come under suspicion was in the Baltic at a place called Peenemunde. Many of the photographs processed at Medmenham showed an airfield with 'ring like' structures and with many other flights over the same area, it was discovered that Peenemunde was the experimental establishment for both the V-1 and V-2 rockets.

One of the photographic interpreters at Medmenham was a lady by the name of Constance Babington-Smith. For some time it had been her job to study the thousands of photographs taken of the Peenemunde and Calais areas and to note anything that appeared 'strange'. Studying a selection that had been taken on 28th November 1943, her eyes focussed on four minute structures, one of which appeared to be a ramp. Though these had been seen on earlier photographs by other interpreters, they had been assumed to be connected with dredging equipment. Constance, however, recognised them as something much more sinister and convinced her superiors at Medmenham that they were ramps for pilotless aircraft. By December 1943, her interpretation had become fact and the sites were subject to relentless bombing by the Allied air forces.

These are but a few of many incidents recorded at RAF Medmenham. Photographic intelligence did play a large part in the final defeat of the enemy for without the 'eyes of the air', victory would have been just that little bit harder to obtain.

19

THE MAGIC OF MILLER

On 24th December 1944, a press release issued by the USAAF at 18.00 hrs was as brief as it was vague.

'Major Alton Glenn Miller, Director of the famous United States Army Air Force Band which has been playing Paris, is reported missing whilst on a flight from England to Paris. The plane in which he was a passenger left England on December 15 and no trace of it has been found since its take-off. Major Miller, one of the outstanding orchestra leaders in the United States, lived at Tenafly, New Jersey, where his wife presently resides. No members of Major Miller's band were with him on the missing plane.'

Although Glenn had disappeared on 15th December 1944, reporting procedures were suspended for nine days. The announcement, however, when it came, began one of the greatest wartime mysteries of the decade and one that rumbles on even today.

In the summer of 1942 Glenn Miller and his civilian band were at the top in popular big bands. Two films had helped them to achieve this fame, *Sun Valley Serenade* shot in 1941, followed by *Orchestra Wives*. The band's radio broadcasts in the USA had pushed their fame even higher with one of the broadcasts in 1941 called *Sunset Serenade* paying tribute to the many American servicemen being drafted at this time. A short time later the Japanese attack on Pearl Harbor was to bring the USA fully into the war.

As America became entrenched in the global war, Glenn disbanded the civilian band in September 1942 and joined the United States Army, being given the rank of Captain. After two months training, Captain Miller was transferred to the Army Air Forces and was given the job of forming a military band.

During the spring of 1943 he put together an orchestra incorporating many of the swing musicians of that period – drummer Ray McKinley, pianist Mel Powell, trumpeter Bernie Priven, clarinetist 'Peanuts' Hucko and many more. This was to be a military band of a different kind! A radio series titled *I Sustain the Wings* was first broadcast over the CBS Network during May 1943. Such was its impact on a jazz-starved public that for nearly a year, Glenn and his band broadcast every Saturday night.

As the build-up to D-Day continued, it was decided that a special radio network should be set up to broadcast once the invasion had begun. The boss of the network, Colonel Edward Kirby, had also been given the task of obtaining an orchestra to broadcast from London to the Allied forces. When approached for advice, Glenn suggested his own orchestra. With approval from General Eisenhower's naval aide, Commander Harry Butcher, it was finalised that Glenn should bring the band to London to do the broadcasts. On 18th June, Glenn and his radio producer, Technical Sergeant Paul Dudley, flew to England whilst the band left New York aboard the *Queen Elizabeth*. They disembarked at Gourock on the Firth of Clyde in Scotland on 28th June, and travelled on the overnight train to London.

Major Glenn Miller fronts his band of the AEF.

Now known as the American Band of the Allied Expeditionary Force, they commenced a gruelling period of broadcasts and live concerts. Fronting a 40-piece orchestra including strings and singers, Glenn could pack a B-17 hangar with GIs twice over. The radio schedule continued throughout 1944 whilst the live concerts continued until 3rd October 1944 when, with an English autumn setting in, the hangars were proving too cold to play. During November, newly promoted Major Miller increased the broadcasts over the AEF network and in late November, told the band that they would be playing concerts in Paris over the Christmas holiday for around '30,000 to 40,000' GIs of the AEF.

With all the arrangements made, Major Glenn Miller and the band gave their last live broadcast at the Queensbury Club in London. Being offered a flight to Paris ahead of the band arriving, Glenn together with a Colonel Baessell, drove to RAF Twinwood Farm in Bedfordshire where a single-engined Norseman aircraft was waiting to take them to Paris. The weather was at its worst, fog and low cloud all over the UK. Despite this, the pilot, Flight Officer Johnny Morgan, assured his passengers that once they got above the fog, it would be fine. The Norseman left Twinwood Farm at 1.55 pm on Friday, 15th December 1944 never to be seen again. It began one of the most fascinating mysteries of the Second World War.

Glenn and the band of the AEF played three venues in Oxfordshire:

> Station 519 – GROVE. On Saturday, 12th August 1944, a
> small jazz group played for a dance at the Officer's
> Club used for the 31st TG.
> Station 234 – MOUNT FARM. On the evening of Monday,
> 25th September 1944, the entire band played a concert in
> the same hangar where Bob Hope had performed a year
> earlier.
> 91st GENERAL HOSPITAL OXFORD. This was an open-air
> concert on the hospital lawn for all patients and staff.

The assumed death of Major Miller in the Norseman was a great loss to music and to the morale of all the fighting men and women. Many suggestions have been put forward as to what actually happened to the aircraft and its passengers. The weather was atrocious and may have caused ice to form on the wings of the aircraft, causing it to crash into the Channel. Another more recent explanation given is that the

Norseman crossed under a formation of Lancasters that were dumping their bombs in an area off Beachy Head after an abortive mission. One of the navigators on one of the Lancasters stated that he saw a light aircraft passing beneath them as they commenced dropping their bombs. Another is that Glenn was not even on the Norseman when it took off but had flown to Paris earlier and was killed in a brawl outside a Paris nightclub. Whatever happened, his death left a legacy of music that is enjoyed by many today and is sheer nostalgia of the period. His signature tune, *Moonlight Serenade*, will just go on for ever.

20
CIVILIANS AT WAR

'I see the damage done by the enemy attacks; but I also see, side by side with the devastation and amid the ruins, quiet, confident, bright and smiling eyes, beaming with a consciousness of being associated with a cause far higher and wider than any human or personal issue. I see the spirit of an unconquerable people.' So spoke Winston Churchill in the House of Commons on 12th April 1941.

The impact of war was felt at home at once. Like the Scout movement, the motto became 'Be Prepared', yet strangely enough, many people were not. Not until the first enemy aircraft appeared in the sky did some of the civilian population wake up to the fact that we really were at war. Then things happened rapidly. The sight of silver barrage balloons in the sky, the advent of the blackout and the evacuation of all the young children, helped to bring about a sense of realisation. From 1939 onwards, the next six years, for civilians, would evoke what became known as the Spirit of Wartime.

In Oxfordshire as elsewhere, however, signs of an imminent war were only too obvious by the late 1930s. The Government in 1938, convinced that if war came Britain would be invaded early on, began to prepare in earnest. The British Ministry of Information were soon at work distributing leaflets telling householders what to do should an invasion occur. The main one titled *If the Invader Comes*, gave the first rule in large black letters:

IF THE GERMANS COME, BY PARACHUTE,
AEROPLANE OR SHIP, YOU MUST REMAIN WHERE YOU ARE.
THE ORDER IS 'STAY PUT'.

Public Information Leaflet No.2 stated: 'In war, one of our great protections against the dangers of air attack after nightfall would be the 'blackout'. On the outbreak of hostilities all external lights and street lighting would be totally extinguished so as to give hostile aircraft no indication as to their whereabouts. The motto for your safety is KEEP IT DARK.'

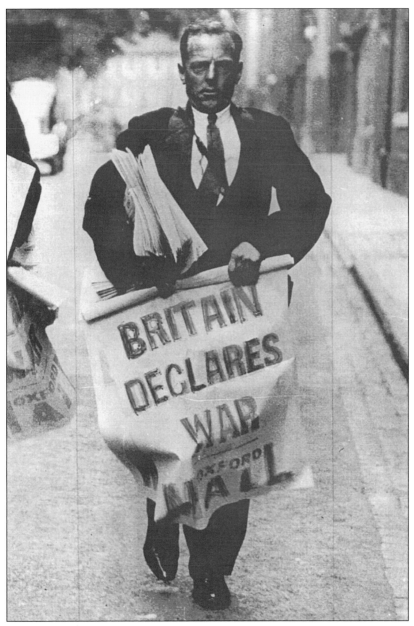

A city news vendor announces the start of the war. (Centre for Oxfordshire Studies)

Of all the wartime conditions, it was perhaps the blackout that had the strongest effect on the nation. Moving about at night became so disorientating and hazardous that most people chose to stay in. Trains and buses were lit by a single bulb whilst cars had hoods over the headlights with just a small slit to allow the beam to shine through. This together with the fact that there was no street lighting caused a doubling of the number of motor accidents in certain areas. The number of casualties reported due to people falling down steps, bumping into posts etc were also on the increase. Any chink of light seen appearing from behind closed curtains was immediately met by a shout of 'Put that light out'. In Oxford and the surrounding towns and villages, a speed limit of 20 mph was introduced. One man found doing over 30 mph and stopped by the police managed to evade prosecution by stating that due to the blackout and the fact that his dashboard was not illuminated, he could not see his speedometer. Reluctantly, the judge accepted his plea and the man was let off!

It was really far safer to draw the blackout curtains properly, stay at home and listen to the wireless. During the hours of darkness this became the only link with the outside world as all cinemas and places of entertainment were closed soon after war was declared for fear of bombs. This at the time was a shame as the residents of Oxford were enjoying Arthur Lucas and Kitty McShane in *Old Mother Riley* at the New Theatre, whilst the Playhouse in Beaumont Street had *The Playhouse Review* starring Leslie French. When the expected onslaught did not happen, some did reopen but for the civilians of Oxfordshire, life had suddenly become very bland.

Also in 1938, 38 million gas masks were issued as the fear of a gas attack became uppermost. People were advised to carry them wherever they went, contained in a cardboard box and tied with string. Children's masks were available together with a self contained unit for babies in which the infant was totally enclosed and was fed air via a hand pump. Even dogs were thought of with a gas mask made to fit over the canine head. Cats were left to fend for themselves as usual. However, by the spring of 1940, with no gas attack and very little action regarding the war, almost no one bothered to carry their masks. This was the period known as the 'phoney war', which was to last until May 1940.

At this time there was still an air of unreality about the war, yet for the Oxfordshire housewife, her daily struggle with ration cards, queues and a shortage of most items, was already becoming commonplace. It

Oxford nearly became 'Little America' with the arrival of the American forces. The photograph shows temporary American signs in the city centre. (Centre for Oxfordshire Studies)

was rationing that was to hit in the first instance. Introduced in January 1940, butter, sugar, bacon and ham were the first to go on ration. The principal diet became potatoes and bread (housewives were even discouraged from throwing away mouldy bread when it could be made into what passed as a 'bread pudding') as neither of these items were rationed, together with fish and offal. Later in the war a points system was applied to canned meat, fish and vegetables. Each item was given so many points whilst each person was given 20 points to last four weeks. With this method, people could choose what to use their coupons for.

The government exhorted everyone to 'Dig For Victory'. People were encouraged to turn their flower beds and lawns into vegetable patches. Recipes and dietary information came in the form of leaflets and advertising recommending highly nutritious vegetables such as carrots, onions, broccoli, cabbage and brussel sprouts. The wartime housewife wasted nothing. More was recycled then than perhaps today, with tins and metal being saved to be reused for tanks and aircraft, bones boiled to help make glue and explosives, kitchen waste made into swill for pigs, and papers going through a recycling process.

The phoney war also allowed time for the distribution of home air raid shelters to protect against bombs and flying shrapnel. The most universal type of domestic shelter was the Anderson, named after the then Home Secretary, Sir John Anderson. Allocation in Oxfordshire was started before war broke out and they were provided free to those earning less than £250 a year. Easily constructed in the garden, they were made of curved steel which was bolted together and had to be dug into the ground and covered with three feet of earth. Apart from being very cold, they were small and were liable to flood. 'Going to the shelter' became a ritual from June 1940 onwards.

The other nationally issued shelter was the Morrison. This was for internal use, usually in the main living room of the house. Rather like a cage, it was constructed of iron on the top whilst the sides were of strengthened mesh. The idea was that you used the top as a table, before going to bed in the cage. Though not as universally accepted as the Anderson shelter, yours truly can vouch for their strength when a V-1 landed near my home in Kent!

It was however the arrival of evacuees in the county that really brought the feeling of war to the community. With the declaration of hostilities, the government immediately authorised the greatest upheaval of the war. Not only were wives saying goodbye to their

Whilst a woman hangs out her washing in an Oxford suburb, the troops mass for the Great Invasion. (Imperial War Museum – ref. NYT27247)

men going into battle, they were mothers saying goodbye to their small children as the evacuation to safer areas took place. The operation was appropriately code-named 'Pied Piper' as the youngsters, complete with small cases, gas mask holders swinging from their shoulders and brown paper labels around their necks indicating their name and address, waited at railway stations in London and the home counties with their mothers. They were usually organised into school groups and were destined for the areas that the nearest main-line station from their homes served. In the case of those bound for Oxfordshire, it was either King's Cross or St Pancras.

Amidst tears and much clinging, the children boarded the trains for the reception areas in the towns and villages they were allocated to. Many arrived at their destination dirty, hungry and homesick. Most of the evacuees for Oxfordshire came from London, a great majority of them never having been to the country before. Some were in need of better clothes, some a good bath and scrub and even some, de-lousing! Many came to a far better standard of living than they had experienced in their own homes and when the time came, did not want to return to their origins.

Although the government had planned to move about 3.5 million people, in the end only 1.5 million families joined the scheme. In September 1939, 827,000 children, 524,000 pre-school children and their mums, 12,000 pregnant mothers and 103,000 teachers and helpers were on the move. However, this first wave of evacuation did not last long, and three out of four children were back home by spring 1940 due to the inactivity of the war. Evacuation would continue throughout the war, but on a smaller scale.

At Buckland, they came from West Ham and were received at the local school by the headmaster and some of his teachers. After being allocated to families, the local people ensured that the frightened and tearful new arrivals were soon made to feel at home by, with the meagre rations they had, managing to make little cakes with icing and distributing them to the evacuees. For these and many other lucky individuals, life did in the end become very exciting in the country.

The village of Hailey was also to see many evacuees. It is recorded that after keeping kettles boiling and beds aired, villagers found that the evacuees did not arrive at the predicted time. However, after several days of suspense, an LCC school unit of about 75 children and five teachers arrived from Hackney. They were eventually billeted in private homes and the Marlborough Hall was requisitioned as a school. A week after their arrival, the Mayor of Hackney paid a visit and gave each child a sixpence before he returned home. Later in the war, more evacuees arrived in Hailey and filled all the available accommodation.

Finstock was another village to feel the effects of evacuees on a small community. Twenty seven children arrived the day before war broke out but difficulties were soon encountered when it was found that the habits of most of them left a lot to be desired. Some of the hosts refused to accept children, who were then accommodated in the village hall. They did not stay long and had all returned to their London homes by Christmas 1939. The second group in June 1940 were from Enfield and were much more acceptable to the good people of Finstock. These villages are but three among many to receive evacuated children, some of whom never returned to London but became used to country life.

Apart from the evacuees, it was the Home Guard that was always there to remind Oxfordshire people of the threat of invasion. With many able-bodied men already in the forces, it became imperative that a home-based military unit should be available if needed. On 14th May 1940, Sir Anthony Eden, Secretary of State for war, broadcast to the nation:

'I want to speak to you tonight about the form of warfare which the Germans have been employing so extensively against Holland and Belgium, namely the dropping of troops by parachute behind the main defensive lines. Since the war began, the government have received countless enquiries from all over the Kingdom from men of all ages who are for one reason or another, not at present engaged in military service. And who wish to do something for the defence of their country. Well, now is your opportunity. We want large numbers of such men in Great Britain who are British subjects between the ages of 17 and 65, to come forward now and offer their service in order to make assurance doubly sure. The name of the new force which is now to be raised will be the Local Defence Volunteers.'

Within 24 hours, 250,000 men had enrolled nationally, this figure rising to more than a million by July. The name did not last long, for in a speech on 23rd July 1940, Winston Churchill referred to the volunteer force as the Home Guard. This name was officially adopted immediately afterwards.

In the beginning the Home Guard were certainly badly equipped to repel an expected invasion. Their only forms of weaponry were pick-axe handles, forks, rakes, the odd First World War gun and a variety of home-made weapons. Of the latter, the Molotov Cocktail was a superb piece of ingenious invention. Consisting of a bottle filled with an inflammable liquid and a rag stuffed into the neck and posing as a wick, the idea was to light the rag and throw the bottle at the enemy. When it hit the ground or object, it exploded violently. Had the invasion occurred, it was suggested that the men climb onto the enemy tanks and drop them down the hatch! Such was the spirit of invention in wartime.

The same can be said about the uniform, which in 1940 was just an armband with the letters LDV emblazoned on it with the standard issue of denims. All of this changed however in 1941 when the standard army battledress became the uniform. At the same time, they were issued with rifles which had been shipped over from Canada and America, and were given live ammunition. Now, if the invasion did occur, at least the Home Guard could look as though they meant business. Over the years, they have become the butt of many jokes with the catchphrase 'Don't panic' from *Dad's Army* becoming a byword. No doubt, though, if Hitler had arrived, they would have given the enemy

An assault course was set up in Jackdaw Lane in Oxford and was used by a battalion of the County Home Guard. (Centre for Oxfordshire Studies)

a run for his money.

What they did do and what was most evident was to boost morale in the cities, towns and villages throughout the country. In the city of Oxford, there was no shortage of volunteers to join the Home Guard. Given the title 'The 6th Oxfordshire (Oxford City) Battalion', one of their duties was to guard vital installations such as gas works, railway stations, factories etc at night. After a day's hard work in their civilian job, it was home to change into uniform and out to man one of the shifts, which might be from 11 pm to 1 am, 1 am to 3 am or 3 am to 5 am, according to the hours of darkness. In between, it was a case of getting your head down and attempting to sleep anywhere. It is interesting to recall several incidents regarding the Home Guard and I quote two here with permission of the Oxfordshire Federation of Women's Institutes:

'The Cassington headquarters of the Home Guard was at the Chequers pub. One man thought that he would get kitted up early

234

and brought a camp bed to sleep on in the pub. This was fine until it came to his shift whereupon he would return about three hours later and find someone else sleeping on it. In one of the exercises the task was to capture Manor Farm. The format was that a single round was to be fired at the commencement of the exercise and another at the finish. When they reached the farm there was no one there to attempt to repel them so they were able to take Manor Farm easily. There was no final shot to signify the end and so they made their way back to the Chequers to find the rest of the group, including the supposed enemy, propping the bar up and the worse for wear!

One other incident was when the Home Guard at one time were responsible for looking after the electricity sub station at Yarnton. At that time there were some Canadian soldiers stationed at Blenheim who considered the local Battalion of Home Guard a joke. Upon being challenged by one of them, one of the Canadians threatened to shoot the guard unless he let him pass. The Home Guard soldier lived to see another day. The Canadians were however considered a wild lot by all the locals. They stole one of the Duke's pigs and roasted it and later on managed to trap a steer,

One of the city ambulance depots manned by permanent crews and the St John Ambulance Brigade. They carried out sterling work. (Centre for Oxfordshire Studies)

giving it the same treatment. By this time the Duke was a little upset at the loss of his stock. After all, the locals, including the Duke himself, were living on coupons whilst the Canadians were living it up. It was duly reported to the law who visited the Canadian camp in the early hours of the morning only to be told that if they had arrived a little earlier, they could have had a piece of real meat!'

It was not only the uniforms of the Home Guard that were seen around Oxfordshire during this period. Others included the Observer Corps, Civil Defence Wardens, First Aid parties and firefighters. In order to keep all these civil defence services ready and on the alert, many combined exercises were arranged during the Phoney War. It is necessary to record but one exercise and incident in order for the reader to appreciate how realistic these were. Again it was the village of Hailey that saw the action. During one particular exercise, it was assumed that incendiaries had fallen on a house in the centre of the village causing fires and destruction. High explosives were purported to have hit the school with many casualties needing the services of the ambulance service and the first aid teams. It gave those villagers not taking part an exciting time! Later in the war, Hailey was subject to an enemy attack when between 500 and 1,000 incendiary bombs were dropped on the west side of the village about 200 yards behind the main street. Luckily most landed in fields but several caused damage to property. The wardens immediately went into action with all the previous exercises ensuring that the operation ran smoothly.

With the fall of France in 1940, as we have seen, the effectiveness of these and similar exercises was soon to be tested in reality. Oxfordshire being away from the main battle area, did not receive the full fury of the enemy but suffice to say, it did suffer its fair share of enemy bombing. It began in the autumn of 1940 when Banbury received an attack, followed by Witney. During the August of that year, leaflets had been dropped by German aircraft over the entire county. The headline ran: 'A last appeal to reason by Adolf Hitler'. In defiance of this, the *Bicester Advertiser* carried the message: 'Keep a good heart, we are going to win through.'

On 3rd October following, Banbury received one of the first attacks in the county. It came in the afternoon when the town was full of people, many going to the cattle market. A Dornier bomber suddenly appeared out of the cloud and dropped his bombs in the vicinity of the marketplace. Whilst none hit the sale yard, several fell into a yard nearby, exploding and throwing pieces of red hot shrapnel in all directions. Six people were killed instantly in the huge explosion, with several nearby suffering severe injuries from flying metal. Further bombs fell on two gasometers near the market, turning them into a blazing inferno with smoke and flame extending high into the sky. With just one gasometer still standing, gas storage capacity was cut by 82 per cent, leaving many homes without heat or cooking facilities. Fires were started elsewhere and damage was also done to the local railway system.

The night of Thursday, 21st/22nd November 1940 was a bad one for Witney. With rain and low cloud in most areas, night activity by the Luftwaffe was on a small scale. Despite the adverse weather conditions, Luftflotte 2 sent 40 aircraft to attack London whilst Luftflotte 3 sent 38 aircraft to bomb Southampton and the Midlands. One aircraft found the town of Witney and dropped two bombs causing widespread devastation but luckily no loss of life. This seems incredible considering most people were in bed at the time of the attack. There were injuries but none too serious. However, 220 houses

Scenes of devastation, as the enemy indiscriminately bombs civilians. (SE Newspapers)

237

Camouflaged and waiting lest the enemy should find out. A typical street scene in 1944. (Hampshire Record Office)

were damaged which the *Witney Gazette* recorded as the 'effects on a town in the Home Counties'. It went on:

'The church had most of its windows blown in or damaged, the adjacent hall, Police Station, council offices suffering equally badly through taking the full force of the blast. The nearby school will be unusable for several weeks. Another bomb exploded near some council houses and cottages, necessitating the evacuation of some of the tenants. A range of buildings nearby took the full force of the second bomb and was utterly destroyed. Many plate glass shop fronts were broken but small panes suffered little damage.'

In Oxford, there were persistent rumours that one of Lord Haw-Haw's sinister broadcasts from Germany had included the words: 'After Birmingham and Coventry, it is the turn of Oxford.' Night after night the people of Oxford waited and dreaded the consequences of such raids but luckily, nothing on the scale of the destruction of the two cities happened. Both the city and the county escaped heavy bombing although isolated incidents did bring both death and destruction. One such time was 22nd March 1941, when 20 bombs were dropped by an enemy aircraft, all of them landing between the Wildsmoor Estate and RAF Abingdon. The attack damaged eleven houses and caused one serious injury. Unfortunately one bomb cut the service pipe of the Oxford Waterworks causing great hardship to many people for some time.

On 9th April, a bomb exploded in the street between Littlemore and Cowley causing a boulder to come through the roof of a house. Luckily the occupant was not in bed at the time. It is fair to say that Oxford was not targeted by the enemy as much as other cities. Even the 'Baedeker' or 'reprisal raids' that were carried out on other places of cultural and architectural value did not include Oxford. Why not has never satisfactorily been explained although the best explanation put forward so far is that had the enemy successfully invaded, Hitler would have considered Blenheim Palace as the seat of government for a Nazi Britain. Another suggestion is that Oxford would have provided a vital communications centre for a conquered Britain.

Workmen making temporary repairs to houses damaged by a bomb in a 'Home Counties Town'. (Centre for Oxfordshire Studies)

A brewery suffered damage when a bomb dropped in its grounds. (Centre for Oxfordshire Studies)

Not every tragedy, however, was due to enemy action. With most of the county's airfields carrying out a training role, it was inevitable that there would be crashes. Some were light, others were bad. For the young boys of the period it was an exciting time, as Mr R. Surman of Witney, then ten years old, recalls:

'I well remember a crash that happened in early 1940. It was a Sunday morning about 11 am and I was in the fields above Witney with a friend. A two-seater aircraft, I think it was a Miles Magister training aircraft, came over and just cleared a line of tall elm trees. The engine was banging away like a car backfiring and it was obviously in trouble. The man in the rear cockpit was standing up and shouting something to the pilot. The plane banked round to the left, over the next field and disappeared from our view. We then heard a loud crash and ran towards the spot.

It had come down two fields away, just south of the A40 not far away from the few houses they call Shores Green. I think it must have touched some trees and gone nose down. Some people from one of the nearby houses were also running to the crash. As we crossed the field, I came upon the body of an airman lying sprawled out on his back. He must have been the one in the rear

240

cockpit and had been thrown out. I had a small pocket mirror with me at the time so I placed it over his nose and mouth. It remained clear and I knew he was dead.

We then ran across to the plane and joined two other people already there. It was blazing furiously and to our horror we saw a man still in the cockpit. No one could get to him because of the heat. We watched from a short distance away as the man's flying suit caught fire. He was soon ringed in a halo of flame yet we could do nothing. Someone from the nearby houses must have phoned the fire brigade because they were soon on the scene. They quickly doused the flames but the plane had mostly burnt away.

The airman in the cockpit still sat there in the burned out shell, a blackened heap. When it had cooled down, the fire chief called out to his men, "You know what has to be done. I want two volunteers." No one responded. He asked again and eventually one man said, "All right, I'll do it." In attempting to extricate the pilot, it all ended in disaster when part of the man's arm was dislodged and came away in his hand. At this point the policeman arrived and his first action was to tell my friend and I to leave the scene. We still watched from a distance but this was a memory and a sight that I have never forgotten.'

Another serious incident happened on 2nd September 1942 and involved an aircraft and its glider from No 2 GTS at Weston-on-the-Green. On the day in question, a Miles Master was towing a Hotspur glider on a training sortie. Having taken off successfully from Weston, they were approaching Witney when both aircraft seemed to lose a lot of height. With the glider pilot realising what was about to happen, he disengaged the tow rope just in time to allow the Hotspur to fly over a local church and crash land a couple of hundred yards away. Sadly, the Master crashed into the spire of St Mary's church in Witney killing the pilot, Sgt Crouch and his passenger, LAC Rodger. Two local residents saw this tragedy unfold, a sight that will forever remain in their memories. Mr P. Fisher of Witney recalls what he saw:

'I was at the time having a tea break, outside my workplace, when I saw this aircraft appear. I knew without any shadow of doubt that it couldn't help but hit the church steeple. I called my workmate but by the time he had reached the door, the damage was done. The plane lost a wing but the glider it was towing

St Mary's church, Witney, with the repair to the steeple following damage by the glider and tug still visible.

managed to slip its tow rope and crashland beyond the church. The plane itself crashed in flames about 75 yards behind the wall adjoining my workplace. By the time I had clambered to the top of the wall it was too late to do anything else but watch the destruction. I am sure I saw an arm waving in the cockpit so I think the pilot was still alive at that time. The glider was later recovered and I think the two occupants survived, though they must have been suffering from shock. I certainly will never forget that fateful day.'

Once again, the then ten year old Mr R. Surman recalls his second tragic incident:

'On the day in question I was in the field of Cogges Hills. A glider came over circling very low, it landed a few yards from me. The pilot jumped out and asked the shortest way back to the town. He said the plane towing him had collided with the church. I ran with him across the fields and up Langel Lane. I took him to the church and could see the top of the spire was missing. The plane was on fire in Mr Marrioto's garden. The glider pilot said his best friend had been at the controls of the plane, but sadly he was killed. The glider remained in Cogges Hills for several days. The army posted a sentry to guard it until it was eventually dismantled and taken away. It really was a dreadful day for all of us in Witney.'

The Hotspur was recovered and went on to serve for another four years. Again, these are but two incidents among several.

The records show that up until the end of February 1944, 224 incidents were reported in the county. No bombs fell in Oxfordshire from August 1941 until three bombs were dropped on Broadwell airfield in April 1944. They did not explode. Of the total number of incidents, 13 were by day, the rest by night. The number of bombs dropped came to 1,111 high explosive, 3,037 incendiary, 28 oil, 10 phosphorus, 7 parachute and 4 V-1 flying bombs. These came to a total of 4,197. There were in addition four cases of enemy aircraft machine gunning the population. The casualties came from 14 incidents. These killed 20 people and injured 59 with 394 buildings either demolished or damaged.

These statistics were the bad side but mention must be made of the willingness of the civilian population to help the war effort. The success of Lord Beaverbrook's National Spitfire Fund in 1940 led to an annual series of War Savings Weeks, the money being used for the acquisition of additional military machines including aircraft. Oxford opened its Fighter Fund set up by the *Oxford Mail* in June 1940 aiming to raise the £5,000 necessary to buy a single Spitfire. By 6th August, it had raised over £1,500. Similar appeals were launched in Banbury and Chipping Norton with the Spitfire Fund at Faringdon carrying the following slogan: 'The RAF will fly the Spitfire, let our district be the buyer.' In due course, a Spitfire, s/n P8345, was purchased and was known as the 'City of Oxford' Spitfire. It joined the many other aircraft that bore presentation names with donations provided by individuals and organisations on a world-wide basis. The scheme eventually gave way to the 'Wings for Victory' weeks.

This chapter has described just a few of the preparations for war and the incidents that the civilians of Oxfordshire suffered during six years of hostilities. Their memories are still very vivid and there are many gravestones in the county's churchyards and cemeteries that bear witness to these events. Whilst the Second World War was of course a military conflict, it also became known as the People's War.

A Spitfire purchased with the money donated by the people of Oxfordshire and named 'City of Oxford'. (Centre for Oxfordshire Studies)

Appendix A

THE MAIN RAF SQUADRONS AND THE USAAF UNITS THAT
WERE STATIONED AT THE OXFORDSHIRE AIRFIELDS
BEFORE, DURING AND AFTER WORLD WAR TWO

ABINGDON
15-24-30-40-46-47-51-52-53-59-62-63-97-98-103-104-106-147-150-166-
167-185-238-242-525.

BARFORD ST JOHN
4-169.

BENSON
21-30-52-58-63-82-103-105-114-140-144-147-150-167-215-267-540-541-
542-543-544.

BICESTER
2-5-12-33-48-90-100-101-104-108-116-118-142-144-217.

BRIZE NORTON
10-24-53-99-115-296-297-511 + The Falcons RAF Parachute Team.

BROADWELL
10-76-271-512-575.

GROVE
174-184.

HARWELL
75-105-107-148-215-226-295-570.

KIDLINGTON
52-167.

MOUNT FARM
140.

UPPER HEYFORD
7-10-18-33-34-40-57-58-76-81-99-105-108-113-122-123-157-158-215-218-
    226.

WESTON-ON-THE-GREEN
2-18-90.

CHALGROVE
30th PR Squadron United States Army Air Force.

GROVE
United States 9th Army Air Force Command.

MOUNT FARM
13th, 14th and 22nd Photographic Reconnaissance Squadrons.

Appendix B

AIRCRAFT AND BASES INVOLVED IN
GLIDER OPERATIONS DURING 1944

SQUADRON	STATION	TUG	GLIDER	COMBINATIONS
OPERATION 'TONGA'				
295	Harwell	Albermarle	Horsa	13
296	Brize	Albermarle	Horsa	8
297	Brize	Albermarle	Horsa	12
570	Harwell	Albermarle	Horsa	12
OPERATION 'MALLARD'				
295	Harwell	Albermarle	Horsa	20
296	Brize	Albermarle	Horsa	20
297	Brize	Albermarle	Horsa	20
512	Broadwell	Dakota	Horsa	18
570	Harwell	Albermarle	Horsa	20
575	Broadwell	Dakota	Horsa	18
OPERATION 'MARKET' – 17th SEPTEMBER 1944				
295	Harwell	Stirling	Horsa	25
512	Broadwell	Dakota	Horsa	22
570	Harwell	Stirling	Horsa	19
575	Broadwell	Dakota	Horsa	24
OPERATION 'MARKET' – 2ND LIFT 18TH SEPTEMBER 1944				
295	Harwell	Stirling	Horsa	3
512	Broadwell	Dakota	Horsa	24
570	Harwell	Stirling	Horsa	24
575	Broadwell	Dakota	Horsa	25

OPERATION 'MARKET' – 3RD LIFT 19TH SEPTEMBER 1944

| 570 | Harwell | Stirling | Horsa | 1 |

TUG SORTIES

Stirling — 515 Sorties
Dakota — 457 Sorties
Albemarle — 224 Sorties

GLIDER SORTIES

Horsa — 1,361 Sorties

Appendix C

GLOSSARY FOR LUFTWAFFE UNITS

Jagdgeschwader – Fighter Units.
Kampfgeschwader – Bomber Units.
Zerstorergeschwader – Long Range Fighter Groups.
Erprobungs Gruppe 210 – Experimental Test Wing 210.
Lehrgeschwader – Instructional/Operational Development Group.
Stukageschwader – Dive-bombing Groups.
Kustenfliegergruppe – Maritime Luftwaffe Units.
Kampfgruppe – Coastal Units.

GLOSSARY FOR GERMAN AIRCREW RANKS

Oberst (Obst) – Colonel.
Oberstleutnant (Obstlt) – Lieutenant Colonel.
Major (Maj) – Major.
Hauptmann (Hpt) – Captain.
Oberleutnant (Oblt) – 1st Lieutenant.
Leutnant (Lt) – 2nd Lieutenant.
Fahnenjunkeroffizier (Fhnjr) – Officer Cadet.
Hauptfeldwebel (Hptfw) – Sergeant Major.
Oberfeldwebel (Ofw) – Flight Sergeant.
Feldwebel (Fw) – Sergeant.
Unteroffizier (Uffz) – Corporal.
Flieger (Flg) – Aircraftsman.

Appendix D

GLOSSARY OF TERMS

AASF – Advanced Air Striking Force.
ADGB – Air Defence of Great Britain.
ASR – Air Sea Rescue.
BAS – Beam Approach School.
DREM LIGHTING – System of outer circle lights leading into flare-path lit at military airfields.
DZ – Drop Zone.
EFTS – Elementary Flying Training School.
E&RFTS – Elementary and Reserve Flying Training School.
ELG – Emergency Landing Ground.
FTC – Flying Training Command.
GTS – Glider Training School.
HE – High Explosive.
HGCU – Heavy Glider Conversion Unit.
HQ – Headquarters.
MU – Maintenance Unit.
OCU – Operational Conversion Unit.
OTU – Operational Training Unit.
PRU – Photographic Reconnaissance Unit.
PSP – Pierced Steel Planking.
RLG – Relief Landing Ground.
RAFVR – Royal Air Force Volunteer Reserve.
SFTS – Service Flying Training School.
SOE – Special Operations Executive.
WAAF – Women's Auxiliary Air Force.
WINDOW – Metal foil dropped to confuse radar image.
W/T – Wireless Telephony.

BIBLIOGRAPHY

The Squadrons of the RAF, James J. Halley, Air Britain 1980
RAF Squadrons, Wg Cdr C. G. Jefford MBE RAF, Airlife 1988
The Battle of Britain – Then and Now, After the Battle 1980
The Blitz Vol 1,2 & 3, After the Battle 1987
Britain's Military Airfields 1939/1945, David J. Smith, Patrick Stephens
    1989
Aircraft of the RAF, Owen Thetford, Putnam 1962
D-Day – Classic Conflicts, Salamander 1999
Victory in Europe, Julian Thompson, Sidgwick and Jackson 1994
1940 – The World in Flames, Richard Collier, Penguin 1980
The Narrow Margin, D. Wood & D. Dempster, Hutchinson 1963
The 1,000 Bomber Plan, Ralph Barker, Pan Books 1967
Strike Hard, Strike Sure, Ralph Barker, Pan Books 1965
There Shall Be Wings, Max Arthur, Hodder & Stoughton 1993
The Spirit of Wartime, Index 1995
Per Ardua Adastra, Philip Congdon, Airlife 1987
Bases of Air Strategy, Robin Higham, Airlife 1998
Action Stations No. 6, Michael J. F. Bowyer, Patrick Stephens 1990
Action Stations No. 9, Chris Ashworth, Patrick Stephens 1985
A Waaf in Bomber Command, Pip Beck, Goodhall 1989
Oxfordshire Within Living Memory, Oxfordshire Federation of Women's
    Institutes, Countryside Books 1994
RAF Edgehill, Eric G Kaye, Self Publishing Assoc 1990
The Battle of Britain, Richard Hough & Denis Richards, Guild Publishing
    1990
Railway Air Services, John Stroud, Ian Allan 1987
The Battle of Britain, Jon Lake, Index 2000
Squadrons of the Fleet Air Arm, Ray Sturvitant, Air Britain 1984
Airfield Focus, Peter Davies, GMS Enterprises 2001
A History of RAF Brize Norton, Steve Bond
They Flew From The Top Of Wykham Hill, David J. Neal

ACKNOWLEDGEMENTS

I acknowledge with grateful thanks all the individuals and organisations who have assisted me in the writing of the book. I list them in no special order.

Flt Lt Richard Jones (Witney); Flt Lt Jim Robson; Major Richard Colvile; Flt Sgt Mick Harris, RAF Benson; RAF Brize Norton; Martin Baker Co Ltd; Department of the Air Force, Air Force Historical Research Agency, Maxwell Air Force Base, Alabama, USA; Imperial War Museum; RAF Museum Hendon; Public Record Office; Banbury Cake; *Bicester Advertiser*; *Henley Standard*; *Witney and West Oxfordshire Gazette*; Mrs Joan Sylvester; Mr Peter Davies; Mr John W. Dossett Davies; Mr Bruce Robertson; Mr Frank Cheesman; Mr R. Surman; Stan and Vivien Warwick; Mr Neil Richards; Mr P. Fisher; Mr P Sirett; Mr Derek Chamberlain; Mavis and Richard Dyson; Mr Colin Cohen; Mr Steve Bond; Mr Eric G. Kaye; Mr Len Pilkington; Centre for Oxfordshire Studies; Oxfordshire Federation of Women's Institutes; Mrs Pip Beck; Mr G Markham; Mr Doug Neil; A. Moor.

If I have omitted to mention any person or organisation or incorrectly credited any photographs, please accept my sincere apologies. Final thanks go to my wife, Barbara, as much for her patience as for her help and correcting.

INDEX

253

RAF Squadrons & Units to 1945

US Photo-Reconnaissance Squadrons